D1241753

COMFORT ME
WITH APPLES

COMFORT ME WITH APPLES

CONSIDERING THE PLEASURES OF THE TABLE

JOE FIORITO

NUAGE
EDITIONS

Cover design by Ramez Rabbat.
Cover painting by Višnja Murgic.
Photo of cover painting by Christian Knudsen.
Photo of Joe Fiorito by Susan Mahoney.

Acknowledgements
These essays originally appeared in slightly different form in HOUR Magazine in 1993-94. Thanks to Martin Siberok and Josey Vogels. For editorial guidance, thanks to Susan Mahoney and Mark Abley. Thanks to my son Matt for his encouragement. Thanks also to my brothers, my aunts, uncles and cousins for their support. Finally, I am indebted to those whose stories I have observed and recorded.

Published with the assistance of The Canada Council and the Quebec Minister of Culture.
Printed and bound in Canada by Les Ateliers Graphiques Marc Veilleux.

Dépôt légal, Bibliothèque nationale du Québec and the National Library of Canada.

Canadian Cataloguing in Publication Data

Fiorito, Joe, 1948–
      Comfort me with apples

ISBN 0-921833-35-0

      1.Food.   2.Gastronomy.   I.Title
TX355.5.F46 1994   641' .01'3   C94-900322-0

NuAge Editions, P.O. Box 8, Station E
Montréal, Québec, H2T 3A5

For Grace and Dusty
and for Susan, without whom…

Stay me with flagons; oh! comfort me with apples,
for I am sick of love.

—The Song of Solomon

CONTENTS

*These stories contain recipes. Go ahead, try them at home!

FEAST OR FAMINE

I saw a kid in grade school eat an apple once. He was a recent immigrant, poor and hungry and more than a little confused. He ate as an animal might, eyes scanning left and then right, ready to defend.

He tore the flesh of the apple with his teeth. He ate it, core and all. And then he saw me looking. As if I'd caught him in a shameful act, he turned away, embarrassed and defiant.

What I saw was the hunger of a lifetime. A hunger which nurtures hatred for those who have full bellies. A hunger which, if you've ever had it, makes you hate yourself for feeling hungry, and distrust those who overeat.

I think of this every time I bite into an apple. It reminds me how precious food is. I eat as close to the core as I can.

I think this must be the same hunger that drove a young Spanish kid to become the Beatle of the bullring in the sixties. And when the money began to roll in, El Cordobes travelled from town to town with his very own *jamón serano*.

He'd hang it from the ceiling of his hotel room, so he could carve a slice whenever he wanted to eat. This was a ham more valuable than currency, more precious than a suit of lights. I've never been that poor, but I've been poor enough to know that lack of money is a bitter spice.

Lately I've been able to breathe a little easier on the subject of my own finances. To celebrate, I bought prosciutto. No, not a package of skinny little slices. I mean, I bought a whole damn prosciutto. From the aptly named Fratelli Porco Lagustoso in Toronto. There were dozens of them hanging from gleaming hooks, each one identically dusty and crusted with black pepper.

And there were even more of them in the spotless back rooms of the shop, keeping company with hundreds of sausages and salamis.

How to choose one prosciutto from hundreds of identical prosciuttos? I stood and stared until one of them spoke to me. I should have hung it from a chandelier, it was so good.

I kept it in the fridge. Instead of carving off slices at random, I ate it with melon; Italians have been doing this since the 1400s, when the Vatican librarian Platina published a book in which he decreed it was okay to eat fruit and meat together.

I ate it with bread, cheese, and red wine on days when it was too hot to cook.

I draped slices fine as silk scarves over a salad of butter lettuce, ribbons of carrot, tomatoes and green onions. The dressing was three tablespoons olive oil, one tablespoon red wine vinegar, one teaspoon balsamic vinegar, a half teaspoon of Dijon mustard and a quarter teaspoon of honey.

I made *involtini*, using thin slices of beef seasoned with rosemary, black pepper and parsley. I added sheets of my pink prosciutto and slices of fontina cheese. I rolled them up, secured them with toothpicks and browned them in olive oil. I set the meat aside, drained off the fat, made a simple tomato sauce in the pan and used that to dress the little bundles. This is spectacularly good with new potatoes.

On days when I was feeling especially wealthy with my prosciutto, I heated a couple of strips in a frying pan and had them for breakfast with eggs. Those were the days when I felt the richest.

Now my prosciutto is gone, and the bone is sitting in the freezer waiting to be cooked with white beans and sage. This is the kind of table I'd set for the kid with the apple and the Spaniard. Just the three of us at dinner. Seconds and thirds if we wanted.

Mopping our plates with the last of the bread.

Our bellies full.

Us, smiling.

THE THEATRE AS PORK CHOP

The price of theatre tickets is sky-high, and the stage is full of actors bellowing to the back of the room. Why do they do that? Noise is no substitute for emotion. Why should I pay hard cash for the privilege of being yelled at?

I say the best, the cheapest theatre, is that which you make yourself. Go shopping, buy a pair of pork chops and call it the Theatre of Hunger.

For the purposes of this drama, you are writer, director and lead actor. Feel free to improvise from the text. What happens is what's happening—be, don't think, and build on that.

Take to the street. The passers-by are your supporting cast. Some steal scenes. Some are hams. Ignore them. Remember why you're hungry. Be your hunger.

Walk until you find a butcher shop. You'll find him there behind the counter. Holding a knife. Waiting for you. Call him Charcutier.

He's spent years preparing for the moment. Consider the blood on his apron, look at his knives, look at the fat white scars on his fingers. Stanislavski said if the eyes are the mirror of the soul, the fingertips are the eyes of the body. He said the slightest tenseness in the fingertips will prevent your entry into the realm of the subconscious.

He meant you shouldn't play with knives.

The subtext of this scene is apparent. Some farmer has spent months raising a noble but doomed pig. It was as familiar to him as the family cat. Like Fluffy, it responded when its ear was scratched. Its fate was sealed from the beginning. Never mind.

It's been stunned, stuck, bled, scalded, gutted; it's been split in half and trucked off, chilled. Now it's chops and cutlets, rosy roasts and ribs in plastic trays. Never mind.

The woman in the line in front of you buys bacon. Her perfume is familiar. Musk stinks. The scent of it invades your nose. She'll leave in a moment. Ignore her. Make the action happen by observing it.

Now is the time. It's you and Charcutier alone on stage. Don't look at the butcher, look at the meat. You may have to force the dialogue.

He may wink at the woman and say, as my butcher did last week, "All the ladies like the way I wrap my meat." You can't do anything about it when she laughs as heartily as he does. But you should be prepared.

He'll say, "May I help you?" or "What'll it be today?" He might say "Puis-je vous aider?" Be prepared. Point to the chops, ask for two and watch the action quicken. He'll take them, weigh them, wrap them in paper and tie them with cord.

He'll ask "Will there be something else?" Make him work with you. Pause and look at the bacon on the counter, look at the slabs of smoked ribs hanging in rows behind him.

Tell him "No."

He'll take your money. He may wish you a pleasant day. He may tell you to come again. Butchers are familiar with the theatre. Marty was a butcher. Ignore him. This is your play, not his. Grasp the chops with feeling, mind and being.

Leave the store at once. The pork chops in your bag are a metaphor for—something. They are your impatience, your appetite, your Holy Grail. Whatever. You're making this up as you go along.

Arrive at your kitchen. Open the package and look at the chops. They are pink and soft. The fat at their edges is surprisingly white, a ribbon of snow. Better than snow, if you look out the kitchen window.

Pour a glass of wine, and curse. This is your theatre, and the men and women of the liquor store are stage hands. They're working behind the scenes for you—but they're unionized, they're better paid than you are, and they have more security. That's why your play costs what it does. Curse them.

Heat a pan. Add two tablespoons of olive oil. Some poor peasant in Italy…never mind, you don't need every little detail. Your motivation is hunger. We're talking method here, not Method. Add a finely slivered clove of garlic to the oil, along with two tablespoons of fennel seeds.

Heat gently in the pan.

Season the chops with salt and pepper. Now sauté them for five minutes on each side. Add a cup of wine, lower the heat, cover the pan and simmer for twenty minutes.

While the chops are cooking, make a small salad. Reheat last night's mashed potatoes. Set your place at the table, according to what is true.

Serve the chops with the sauce from the pan. Sprinkle with chopped parsley. Fill your glass again, and light the candles.

Open the latest reviews. Read what they're saying about Michel Tremblay. Where are *Les Belles-Soeurs* now? Hoot, lassie, last time I looked they were in Scotland. Never mind.

You enter the final scene, an actor eating chops.

The audience is watching.

MY FRIEND BERNARD

The guest is a jewel resting on the cushion of hospitality. The host is king, and should not condescend to a lesser role.

This may be an aphorism from the heights of some once-great Balkan country. It may be simply something that Rex Stout stuck in the mouth of his fictional detective, Nero Wolfe. No matter. The sentiment bears scrutiny.

It requires the host to assume a sweeping and dignified set of obligations. And it requires the guest to maintain a posture of worthiness. After all, one who acts like a boor in another's house can hardly be considered a jewel on a cushion; some other substance, perhaps.

But there are some situations where no aphorisms apply, and you must always remember that a writer as a guest is a spy and a snitch, not a jewel.

Consider what I'm about to tell you of my friend Bernard. He is a bear of a man, generous with his friends and open of heart. He is a man of wild appetite, in love with whatever is on his plate, and hungry for the company of his companions.

I've had occasion to stay with him once or twice. He is no housekeeper. Old newspapers mingle with equally old socks on the floor by his couch. Mould is no stranger to the back of his fridge or the inside of his shower curtain. And you don't have to be a detective or a nutritionist to reconstruct the meals of the past week. A glance at his stovetop is enough.

But Bernard is fastidious with books and friends, and a man who treats these carefully can be forgiven many sins.

I used to eat cretonnes at breakfast with Bernard, until the day the white stuff on the surface turned out not to be pork fat. White mould looks pretty on cheese, but it tastes like hell on meat.

But what really threw me off my feed was the morning I woke early and decided to take a quick shower. The coast was clear. Bernard was in his room, snoring like a trooper. I headed for the bathroom.

When I emerged from the shower, I discovered he had risen. He was standing at the kitchen sink, wearing the dashiki he used as a nightshirt. He was standing on tip-toe. His back was turned to me.The front of the dashiki was hiked up around his waist.

Bernard was peeing in the sink.

I made it to my room before he finished. He didn't hear me. I was silent, speechless. Much as I like Bernard, I decided then and there I'd never wash a head of lettuce in that sink again.

Bernard and I have a mutual friend, a CBC vice-president. Call him Gerald. He, too, stayed some weeks with Bernard. Like me, he met all of Bernard's separatist pals and spent time in the company of his wonderful former lovers. Gerald and Bernard drank wine and argued politics all night long.

Sometimes they ate together in restaurants, but Bernard is not a wealthy man. He economises on occasion, and sometimes cooks at home.

Like many men unfamiliar with the finer points of cuisine, if not the finer points of knives, Bernard cooks with a flourish, and he takes it surprisingly hard when he learns you don't enjoy eating what he cooks.

Once, while making a bowl full of salad at the sink (the self-same sink!) Bernard cut himself with a knife.The cut was sharp and bright, and Bernard swore. He licked his finger once, then ran the wound under the tap. The flow of water was red, then pink.

Gerald, busy sorting the socks from the newspapers, saw what happened. Are you cut very bad, he asked. Not too very bad, replied Bernard in his deep voice. He continued slicing things into the salad. And Gerald watched as drops of blood splashed brightly on the leaves of lettuce in the bowl, along with the olive oil and the vinegar.

There are times when a good guest says nothing, and pushes aside his lettuce or his cretonnes; there are times when all a good guest can do is smile as warmly as a jewel while the light falls through the kitchen window; then, the good guest steps down from the cushion of hospitality and says simply "Hey, Bernard. Come on. Supper's on me downtown."

A Christmas Present

One day last summer, while channel-surfing, I saw a group of little campesinos and campesinas. They were young kids, perhaps ten or eleven years old. The boys wore burnt cork moustaches. The girls had paper flowers in their hair. They were on the ethnic channel, dancing hard.

Barefoot, the girls spun in circles; their dresses billowed around their feet. The boys stood expressionless, arms folded on their chests. They stamped their heels on the studio floor while the girls whirled tightly around them.

The dance looked serious; children are rarely carefree imitating the courtship rituals of their elders. But at the same time, there was a pleasing earnestness about them. These kids were hanging onto their culture with their fingernails. And I knew that somewhere there were grandmothers in black gathered around televisions, eyes moist with visions of youth and home.

But for some reason, as the children danced, I began to think of Christmas. I had no idea why. It was hot and sunny and we were months from snow. I stared at the screen, looking for Yuletide clues. The cat lay in a puddle of sunlight on the floor and switched her tail.

Then the dancing stopped, and I looked at the TV more closely. There seemed to be an imitation mountain in the background. Some clever set designer with limited means had draped a large grey blanket around a conical frame. It resembled a volcano. Its peak was crusted with white paint. From deep inside, billows of fake smoke curled upward and disappeared in the studio air.

And then the penny dropped.

The blanket volcano had the shape of the shortbread my mother used to make at Christmas. She'd form a piece of dough into a cone around a candied cherry. When the shortbread cones were baked, she'd ice the tops with frosting. They looked, I now realized, like little Latino volcanoes. Although that was not her intention.

I used to get boxes of them in the mail at Christmas the first few years after I left home. Now I make my own shortbread, though I've rarely tried to shape it into cones. Which is to say, I tried a couple of times, but I didn't get anything that looked like volcanoes or any other kind of shortbread mountains. I got shortbread molehills.

However you shape them, the basic recipe is simple. Combine a pound of butter with a pound of potato flour, a cup of fruit sugar and three cups of flour until thoroughly blended. Use your hands if you wish. You don't have to be shy with this stuff.

Roll the dough on a floured surface until it's a half-inch thick. Cut into the traditional shapes...angels, Christmas trees, anything you like. Dot with candied peel or not.

Bake in a 300°F oven for about half an hour. Watch closely; bake only until the bottoms of the cookies are faintly brown. Cool on racks. Let them age in a tightly covered cookie tin for a week or so. Eat them by the light of the tree on Christmas Eve.

Just so you know what you're in for, I once gave this recipe to a friend. She made a batch and brought them to a Christmas party where she worked. Her boss, a British person, said they were "Melting Moments."

Those are not necessarily the words I would have chosen. Nevertheless, it is a serious compliment. Properly done, these cookies do melt in your mouth. They are slightly sweet and slightly nutty in flavour, and excellent with a glass of sherry or cognac. One warning—shortbread goes from your lips directly to your hips. Eat in moderation.

These cookies are evocative enough to send me from Latin America in the summer to my mother's kitchen at Christmas. Shortbread for me is a means of transport, as powerful as the madeleine was for Marcel Proust.

Although I'd like to point out that if Proust had been a canoeist instead of an aesthete, and he'd got cookies from home in the mail, then the old song "Paddlin' Madeleine Home" would have an entirely different meaning. He'd have been paddling shortbread home, don't you think?

It's the Knife, Mack

They say only the dull knife cuts your hand, but the truth is it's only a dull knife that cuts your hand by accident.

My Uncle Dominic delivered meat for a butcher when he was a boy. Dom's bicycle carrier was always filled with cold and heavy packages wrapped in butcher paper, and tied with butcher knots.

One morning Dominic came to work and found the butcher sitting in the sawdust on the floor. The man's knife was still in his hand, but the sawdust was red and wet where he sat. His head was slumped forward. His last cut had been short and deep, and informed by a sad knowledge derived from his work. He'd known what he was doing.

Look at your butcher. Count the scars on his hands if you can, and see which of his fingers have lost their tips. Look for a ridge of callous on the edge of the forefinger, near the knuckle; this comes from using a kind of golf grip on the cleaver. These are the souvenirs of flesh preparing flesh.

You have to wonder what a butcher thinks as he washes up.

Alina Reyes writes "The butcher who talked to me about sex all day long was made of the same flesh, only warm, sometimes soft, sometimes hard; the butcher had his good and inferior cuts, exciting and eager to burn out their life, to transform themselves into meat. And my flesh was the same."

The hand that shaped her desire had itself been hotly shaped, and I say a butcher's hands are handsome the way a boxer's nose is, or a ballet dancer's foot—the harder the work, the more dignified is the beauty of the worker.

The pain of a cut hand is unlike any other, marked as it is by a flickering moment of numbness, then a stinging flood of hurt and a feeling of rushed and irretrievable stupidity. Still, I manage to cut myself with a careless frequency. Last year, having opened my presents in the morning by the tree and then my finger in the afternoon preparing the supper carrots, I was forced to eat Christmas dinner with one hand.

Pierre Franey says that if a knife is to fit—not the use of that word, fit—the point of balance must be high up near the handle. As a result, a good knife tends to fall handle first on the floor. This saves the blade, and offers an additional advantage to the superstitious—a knife which falls point first foretells death. You are supposed to be able to ward off death by waving the dropped knife three times over your head.

Imagine walking in on a kitchen filled with superstitious chefs, some of whom have just dropped knives, and some of whom have spilled salt—oh, the furious slashing of blades overhead, and the tossing of salt in the air.

Mystery writer Nicolas Freeling, who worked as a chef before he turned to crime, writes that in professional kitchens, where speed is everything, the chef in a hurry will often cover a nick with a slip of carrot. You're not supposed to cut towards your hand, but when Freeling worked as a chef, he says the ball of his thumb was a cross-hatched pad.

Let me remind you to be careful—stir with a knife and stir up strife. And be careful around the campfire—toast your bread upon a knife, you'll be poor all your life; alternatively, you'll never have a wife. You choose which is the deeper poverty.

If you find a knife, leave it where it lies. It foretells disappointment. And finally, never cross your knife and fork on the plate after eating; misfortune is supposed to result—although in some circles, a crossed knife and fork on a plate is a signal to the waiter that you've finished eating.

SYMPHONY OF SHRIMP

There was a minor war in the workplace. I was new on the job, new in town and without much local knowledge. I was suspect because of my newness, and unsure of who to back. Some people thought I was a plant, and no one wanted much to do with me. Not until she took me in hand and bought me dinner.

It was an act of courage and kindness, delivered one evening in an airy, California-style café. She ordered shrimp with an adoba sauce made of ancho chilis, and a salad of wild rice, smoked bacon, cashews and spring onions in a vinaigrette. I followed her lead. Our waiter brought cold beer, and we talked easily.

But a curious thing happened when dinner was served. She started to eat, and as she ate, she hummed. No discreet little "mmm's" of appreciation, these were melodic, operatic hums which rose and fell with each mouthful of shrimp. Ariatic hums which seemed to break like surf with every sip of beer. These were hum dingers.

I wasn't sure what to do. I thought for a moment I should hum, too. Then I thought that might be ridiculous, a mockery, like mispronouncing esses to a lisper. In the end, I did the only thing I could. I ate my supper cheerfully and pretended to hear nothing.

The shrimp were good enough to mop up after with a piece of bread. Over coffee and dessert I learned where the hot spots were at work, how best to avoid them, and who my enemies were likely to be. Her advice was invaluable.

But ever since, when I eat shrimp, I hear her hum.

No one else of my acquaintance has ever made that kind of noise at table. All the while I was growing up, we got whacked for making noise when we ate. Humming would not have been tolerated, although my old man's a passionate musician who loves to eat; I think dining with the hummer would have confused him.

We all have peculiarities at the table. I grew up in a mill town years ago, when it was normal to eat in restaurants whose booths were screened with curtains. I was never sure why this was, until the day I peeked inside another booth. A waiter had opened the curtain to serve one course and clear away another. Some poor bush worker was eating alone. No hums came from him. The noises he uttered were gruesome snarfs and smacks and licks.

His chest was draped in a napkin. He was shovelling food into his mouth, partly with his fork and partly with his fingers. I understood at once. The purpose of the curtain was to hide him from the sight of other diners, and to save him any embarrassment he or we might feel because of his lack of manners.

I thought the curtain was a sad device. At the time, it never occurred to me that for those dining *à deux*, the curtain might hide other equally noisy behaviour, some of which also required the use of the lips and was best kept screened from children.

Curtain aside, few of us are elegant with our mouths agape. And few of us, when dining alone, observe the niceties of custom; we make all the succulent, smacking noises we want. Convention, after all, is meant to govern us in groups.

The woman who hummed at dinner had a partner. I invited him for supper one night, after she'd moved away and before he went to join her. He was a pretty normal guy. Except at the table.

He'd learned to hum from her.

POTATOES TO DIE FOR

We grew potatoes in the garden at home, and naturally some summers they were prone to infestation. Before I got old enough to protest, my job was picking the potato bugs by hand, collecting them in a tin can, and pouring boiling water on them. An ecologist before my time, I learned that life was unfair by drowning insects.

The American gangster John Dillinger had more reason to be fond of potatoes than I ever did. He broke out of jail with one. He carved it into the likeness of a pistol and dyed it black with shoe polish. Mom was right—bad things happen when you play with your food.

History doesn't record what kind of spud Dillinger used. It's a fair question. Had he been a member of the Purple Gang, he might have wanted to carve a purple spud. When I saw potatoes that colour for the first time in a specialty market last week, I immediately bought enough to make a meal for two.

They had wine-coloured skin, and their flesh was dark as amethyst at midnight. They were heavy as jewels in the hand, and I cut deep facets in them with my knife and held them up to the light. They seemed to glow.

When I boiled them, the water turned inky, as if I'd dropped a fountain pen in the pot. I drained them and mashed them with milk and butter, but their colour made for a kind of dissonance at the table. I knew they were food. I knew I was hungry. But picking up my fork was a purely intellectual exercise.

I served them with double-smoked ham, black at the edges and pink inside. Also on the table was a plate of yellow corn bread studded with dried cranberries. The cranberries were a New Year's

Eve purchase, bought on a whim. I wasn't sure what to do with them, so I tossed them in the cornbread batter. Our plates were nothing if not colourful. In case you were wondering, purple potatoes taste a lot like white ones.

Leftovers are usually a happy burden for me—the cornbread disappeared the next morning at breakfast, the ham did its duty in sandwiches, and the hambone was earmarked for a pot of black bean soup.

But the leftover spuds sat in the fridge for a couple of days before I mustered up the nerve to heat them in the frying pan. They looked like something a four-year old would play with at the day care. Normally when my leftovers are blue, it's time to throw them out, but I suppose I could learn to like these.

Unfortunately, agribusiness has no imagination, and we're being cheated by the burger chains. I want that kid in the paper hat, when he asks if I'll have fries with that, to ask "Purple or white ones, sir?"

When someone in a burger joint lights a cigarette after eating fries with ketchup, try to remember that the tobacco plant, the tomato plant and the potato plant are all related. Seen in this light, smoking may be dimly logical, even if it is a crime at least as bad as Dillinger's.

You're supposed to be able to cure rheumatism by putting a potato in your trouser pocket. As it shrinks, it draws the illness out. Maybe this is why people thought the humble tuber was a provoker of lust—is that a potato in your pocket, or are you just glad to see me? Which gives new meaning to the lyrics of the song. I only have eyes for you.

I'm sorry. Let me make it better.

For potato salad, boil half a dozen waxy ones in their skins, in heavily salted water. Drain, then peel and slice while warm. Toss with a handful of chopped scallion, a handful of chopped parsley, half a cup of olive oil, salt, pepper, three tablespoons tarragon vinegar and a splash of white wine. Keep warm. Serve with poached garlic sausage.

Maybe this was what Dillinger was after when he busted out of jail.

PITCHING WOO WITH SOUP

There are no rules about what to serve when you're feeding your date at your place for the first time. But bear in mind that you ought not to serve thin soup if you're nervous. Thin soup falls too easily off the spoon. It's too hard to eat. Serve thick soup instead— nothing is more comforting, or more forgiving to a spoon held in a shaky hand.

Confidence is born of good planning. Here are your directions.

The day before dinner, rustle up a pot big enough for a chicken and five quarts of water. You'll need a large stewing hen. A tablespoon of salt. More ground pepper than you think you need, which is to say as much as you think is enough, and then some more. Add an onion studded with two cloves. A couple of carrots, and the same amount of celery as carrots. A fistful of parsley. A teaspoon of thyme, and maybe some rosemary. A teaspoon of soya sauce if you have it—it helps the colour of the finished product.

Here's a surprise. Add a tablespoon of vinegar, so the calcium from the chicken bones isn't boiled away. Trust me on this. It's a nutritionist's trick, nobody will ever taste the difference, and you'll be eating just a little healthier than the next person. So will the person you're feeding. That's love, no?

Bring everything to a boil. Reduce the heat. Let it simmer. Relax. Think of what you'll talk about at dinner. You may not be a sparkling conversationalist, but you want to be up on things. Read what's on the news stands, read a book.

Six hours pass. The stock is ready. Strain into another pot, ladle it into quart jars, and skim off most, but not all, the fat. Now put the jars in the fridge. The fat that remains will congeal into a nice yellow cap overnight, one that's easy to remove and discard.

28

On the day of your date's arrival, buy a fresh baguette and two small slivers of pâté, and maybe a fruit tart for dessert.

Now you're ready to prepare supper. Take a couple of jars of the chicken stock out of the fridge, and remove the congealed fat. Heat some of the fat in a pot over medium heat, and throw the rest of the fat away.

Add a finely chopped onion and a clove of garlic, also minced. When they're soft, add the broth and bring it to a boil. Toss in a good handful of rice. When the rice is done twenty minutes later, throw in a grated carrot for colour, and add a couple of tablespoons of chopped parsley.

There you are. Supper's ready. Chicken soup with rice, thick enough to hold the spoon. Serve with the baguette, some decent butter, the pâté, a small salad. To wit, to woo. With a glass of wine and dessert, you've dined well, and you aren't so stuffed that you can't think clearly. Your senses are alert for whatever follows.

A note for the advanced. You can toss all the makings of the broth in a pot the night before, bring it to a boil, reduce to the barest simmer, and go to sleep. In the morning, you'll have broth with a delicate, roasted flavour and an amber colour that will win you more than compliments.

While you dine, bear in mind that some people never seem hungry, never seem to pay attention at all to how food tastes. Be on your guard. In the long run, anyone who isn't hungry isn't worth your time.

Here's one consolation. Your love may turn out badly, but you will always have a couple of quarts of broth. Soup will, in the final analysis, comfort you better than a lover.

One last thing. Don't slurp unless you're by yourself.

Breakfast in Bed

The Inuit greet face to face, but they don't rub noses, exactly, and you shouldn't call it kissing. It is a form of greeting every bit as intimate as a kiss, but it goes deeper than that; it's a way for friends to take in each other's smell. It's how friends fill the empty places caused by absence.

Smell is fundamental to happiness. I know a man who travels with a piece of his wife's clothing sealed in a plastic bag. When the separation is too much to bear, he opens the bag and breathes.

Traces of this signature mark our sheets and pillows; this is what makes crawling into bed on a cold night such a comfort.

Smell is one of the many nameless things you miss when love goes wrong. That smell will linger, it will haunt you and exhaust you long after your lover has gone.

Think I'm exaggerating? Wake early one Sunday and smell the person sleeping next to you. Do it. Lean over. The side of the neck will do, just below the ear. Take a deep breath. The knowledge of this scent is lodged in the deepest part of your brain.

Breathe deeply, if only to remind yourself of why you are where you are, doing what you're doing.

Now go into the kitchen. Throw two eggs into a bowl with a cup of milk and a cup of flour. Add a quarter teaspoon of salt and a tablespoon of melted butter. Mix until smooth, but don't overdo it.

Pour the batter into buttered muffin tins, filling the cups no more than half-full. Put the tins in a cold oven. Turn on the heat to 450°F. After fifteen minutes, turn the oven down to 350°F. Wait for fifteen minutes more.

This recipe comes from the *Fannie Farmer Baking Book* by Marion Cunningham. It's an important book, with clear recipes and much new thinking. For example, prior to Marion, popovers were always started in a hot oven. This is a small thing, but one which changed my life.

While you're changing yours, make some coffee and squeeze a couple of oranges. Do what you want with a pear or a pineapple. Get a tray ready to take back to bed.

Now open the oven. It will make you smile. They don't call these things popovers for nothing. They look like little domes, golden brown and slightly crisp on the outside. The texture inside is as soft your partner's neck. The smell is just as warm and every bit as earthy.

Take them out of the muffin tins and put them in a basket. They'll steam as you break them open. Eat them with a little butter and the best jam or honey in the cupboard. A soft camembert isn't out of place if you have it.

Breakfast together is the second or third most intimate thing you can share. If someone new is sleeping over and you want to make an impression, make these. If you're worried about what to talk about while you're eating, remember what Oscar Wilde said. Only dull people are brilliant at breakfast.

If you haven't got a partner, make popovers anyway. It's easy enough to cut this recipe in half. It's good practise. It's its own reward. The butter melts into the jam and the sun pours onto your breakfast bed. And you have another way to fill the emptiness caused by absence.

THIEF OF HEARTS

Maybe it was Dog's idea, maybe it was mine. At any rate, he had the edge on me. His father was a fireman and his uncle was a fat Monsignor whose voice was always hoarse from yelling every Sunday from the pulpit.

If anything went wrong, fire trucks would come to rescue Dog, and his fat uncle the Monsignor would give him some Hail Marys. He could play with hellfire, but he wouldn't get badly burned. My old man delivered the mail. If I got caught, I was going to jail.

Dog and I were in the supermarket, stealing candy. He was after caramels. I was after something else. Valentine's Day was near, and the place was lousy with hearts. Cinnamon hearts, red-hot hearts, the kind that burn your tongue.

The theft was smooth. As if I were invisible, I snatched the biggest bag of hearts I could and stuffed it down my jacket just like that. If you blinked, you missed it. And everybody blinked but me.

I shoved my hands deep in my jacket pockets to keep the loot from falling out. We passed silently by the women at the check-out, but the blood was pounding in my ears and I swear the bag of hearts made a crackling noise, like something burning next to me. Something like the flames of hell. I bolted for the door.

Dog followed me.

When we were safe—a block away, with no-one on our tail—we ate our fill of candy and watched for the cops. I ate some caramels and Dog ate some hearts, as if to share more deeply in the crime. If I was going to hell, I didn't want to go alone.

Supper that night was uneventful, even if the aftertaste of cinnamon ruined the taste of my fish. I took little bites and kept my head down.

Afterwards, I forced myself to finish off all traces of the evidence. I crunched a hundred tiny hearts between my teeth and considered what I'd done. Ash Wednesday was near. I'd have to go to mass and take communion. If I didn't, there'd be questions. I was in a state of mortal sin.

There was only one thing to do.

Dog's uncle, the Monsignor, wasn't in the confessional. That was lucky. The priest on duty said he'd give me absolution. On one condition. I'd have to make restitution. I told him I had no money. He said I'd have to earn some. I asked if I could take communion in the meantime. He said yes, if I swore to pay my debt and said a million prayers.

Jesus.

I took communion gingerly. As if the priest knew why my tongue was red. As if the Sacred Heart of Jesus were made of cinnamon, and I'd stolen that.

Third graders rarely have money, and saving my soul took weeks. But I scraped together all the returnable bottles I could find, and when I had enough I cashed them in. And I cut some slits in a piece of shirt cardboard and filled the slits with coins.

The note to the supermarket man said this: "I stole a bag of candy from your store. I hope you forgive me. Here's the money. I promise not to steal again." I tried to disguise my handwriting. I didn't want anyone tracking me down. I was smart when I was eight.

I probably had to swipe the stamp to mail the envelope, but swiping a stamp isn't a sin if your old man delivers the mail. At least, I didn't think so.

When I told Dog what I'd done to pay my debt, he looked at me like I was a sap. To hell with him. I was clean. I still am. Today, there isn't any supermarket in the country I can't enter with confidence, and there isn't a cashier I can't look in the eye.

There Once Was a Union Maid

It was early in the relationship, so early that neither one of us could have said that there even was a relationship yet.

We were in town to plot union strategy in advance of negotiations. She was representing Prince Edward Island, and I was representing Saskatchewan. We hadn't seen each other for months, and we shared certain feelings.

It was the time of possibility, of shy looks and darting glances, but we had work to do on behalf of another kind of union, and we were working long hours in a stuffy boardroom on a weekend.

As the day dragged on, we got giddy. After we'd figured out how to smash the state, destroy the bosses and free the workers, we were all going out to dinner. She and I were hoping to sit beside each other.

We were discreet. None of our colleagues knew anything was brewing. On the way to the restaurant—there were seven of us—we managed to walk side by side and a little apart from the others. We kept the conversation light and ambiguous, hoping that something might develop over, and after, dinner.

But somehow in the restaurant, between the removal of coats, the ministrations of waiters and the awkwardness of a lot of little tables pushed together to make room for us, we ended up sitting far apart, talking to other colleagues about the state of the membership in the various locals around the country.

We shrugged and smiled at each other. There was nothing to do but order from the menu and dig in.

Digging in isn't easy when you're on a per diem provided by your fellow workers. Union consciousness requires you to keep your expenses down. If you want to eat well at supper, you have to skip breakfast and eat a cheap lunch. I'd done both, and I was starving.

I ordered the wild boar pâté, a honey and wildflower salad, and the buffalo loin with a sauce of gin and juniper, with good beer to wash it down. I looked at her between bites and smiled my Joe-Hill-as-Romeo smile.

I'm a hearty eater, but she ate lightly, a modern girl's supper of consommé and salad and water. I mopped my plate with a piece of bread, and wondered if this was a sign. Maybe she's just not hungry, I thought. And nothing happened then.

Months passed, giving us time to think. When we met again, we were more forward with each other, and clearer in our intentions.

The first night I stayed over at her place, I was surprised by the presence of half a dozen different newspapers on the breakfast table. This is the most pleasant aspect of life with a journalist—breakfast on a sunny morning with fresh newspapers.

There was also some fruit in a pretty bowl—girls' apartments are like that. She'd made the coffee thick and black and I was feeling very pleased with myself. *Après l'amour*, most people are *triste*. In my dictionary, *triste* falls somewhere between "peckish" and "I could eat a horse."

She offered me a bagel. I asked for some butter. She turned the page of her newspaper and said, with a hint of disdain, "Butter?" It was both a question and a statement. I understood it to mean "Lips that touch butter will never touch mine."

"Oh," I said.

I thought I might make a joke of it. Instead, I looked in the fridge to see if there was any marmalade. There was a bale of cauliflower, broccoli, bottled water, and one small pot of farmer's market jam. No bacon. No sausages. Nothing that could be described as hearty.

I reminded myself that her position on benefits for contract workers was the correct one, and I kept my mouth shut. We've been together ever since.

And I'd say we've made great progress as a couple. She's helped me become more even-tempered and more relaxed. I now understand that the state isn't smashed in a day.

As for my effect on her, the other night I found her pouring melted butter on some popcorn, which she then sprinkled liberally with grated parmigiano-reggiano at $12.00 the pound. You've come a long way, baby.

Food Fight

It begins with the pie in the face. Classically, banana cream is the weapon of choice. Other pies are thrown, but anything that's funny is funnier with a banana.

Remember that, from a technical point of view and for the purposes of accuracy, a pie in the face is not literally thrown; more properly, it is pushed flush against the kisser and rotated right-left-right. The slower the better.

The reasons for this are as plain as the meringue-covered nose on your face. Banana cream is fluffy and gluey. Once flung, it tends to stay flung. There's more for the recipient to lick.

Licking is reckoned by observers to heighten the humour.

Call me old-fashioned, but I say times have changed for the worse. Who takes the trouble to bake a pie to throw? And who has the money to buy one from a baker just to slap on someone's chops?

As a result, the modern, post-Stooge *tarte au visage* is licked off at one's peril. What passes for pie is usually nothing more than edible oil from an aerosol can or, only slightly worse, shaving cream whooshed from a nozzle into a pile on a paper plate.

Given the choice, and a certain amount of compassion for your target, throw a pie made of shaving cream. While it will taste marginally worse than Reddi-Whip, it is ounce for ounce the nutritional equivalent of whipped topping, and it does have one advantage. It's soap. It washes out.

I worked for the advertising agency that handled Reddi-Whip when it arrived on the Canadian market. I was still a kid, just another office flunkey with a smart mouth. One day, while chatting pleasantly with one of the account execs, I mentioned with a certain amount of hip and youthful sarcasm that "Reddi-Whip" had a sadistic sound. I went further, and suggested a campaign of spokesmodels in black vinyl, music like the theme from "Rawhide" and plenty of pies in the face.

"Splat" went my career in advertising.

This business of food as a weapon of play is a North American idea whose roots lie in plenitude—we'll never starve here, we have so much food we can waste it on silliness. We can fool around with our food all we want, and still have enough for everyone to eat.

The pie in the face also speaks to a cherished democratic ideal—we're all equal, especially when we're equally stupid. As is a child in a highchair, smearing itself with creamed carrots. Grinning like an idiot.

This, too, is North American, and deeply rooted in the culture. When we are humiliated by smears of food, we're supposed to grin. Should your dinner date misconstrue what you've said, and you sit there with soup on your head or spaghetti in your lap, above it all and underneath it all, you are required to smile urbanely. You may also wish to appear sheepish. This is good form, especially if the incident is your fault.

But you're not supposed to make a fuss. You're supposed to pay the bill and leave. Quietly and alone. With all the dripping dignity you can muster. After leaving a tip for the waiter and the busperson.

It's the same with the pie in the face. You just have to take it with good grace.

I have no idea why this is so. Where I grew up, aggression from any source was greeted with retaliation. Escalated hard. Everybody was kept honest, through a kind of mutual assured destruction.

I should point out that my own experience is limited to witnessing a stack of pancakes snatched off a plate and pushed into a freshly shaved face, with force, at five o'clock in the morning. Don't ask.

You may take my word for it that maple syrup is hopeless as a cologne, unless you wish to attract flies, and it dries too hard to be of any use as a starch for shirts. Lesson learned. A man is simply supposed to change his shirt and leave.

Unless he's got a can of Reddi-Whip, and his aim is true.

Chili Dogs

"He wore a shaggy borsalino hat, a rough grey sports coat with white golf balls on it for buttons, a brown shirt, a yellow tie, pleated grey flannel slacks and alligator shoes with white explosions on the toes."

That's how Raymond Chandler introduces Moose Molloy on the first page of *Farewell, My Lovely*. I don't own clothes as sharp as those, and I'm sure as hell no thug. But when I'm home eating by myself, I like food that makes the same sort of statement—give me chili dogs, which are to normal food what two-toned alligator shoes are to footwear.

I make mine with left-over homemade chili. Whenever I make a pot, I stick some in a little jar and put it in the freezer. You have to have real chili for a chili dog, and the tinned stuff won't do. What are you, a wise-guy? The tinned stuff is dog food.

On the subject of dogs, I use a toulouse or a frankfurter or a weisswurst in a pinch, but never a sausage with paprika. No scrawny Merguez. And never a hot dog from a supermarket. What you really want are long, fat wieners from a real butcher.

Whatever you buy, put a pair of them in a pan of water and bring them to a boil. Slowly. Remove the sausages and put them in a lightly oiled pan. Heat them gently until the skin is crisp. You want a chili dog to burst when you bite into it.

You need raw chopped onion. And yellow mustard, ballpark mustard. The sulphur-coloured stuff, not the Grey Poupon. We're eating chili dogs, not *saucisses*.

You might think you need to put this in a soft bun, the kind you get in the supermarket. You don't. You want a fresh baguette, something which won't fall apart if you steam it, something that's sturdy enough to stand up under a decent sausage and a load of chili.

I know I've been using the term hot dog. Maybe that's wrong. The marriage of wiener and bun is attributed to a German butcher in St. Louis named Feuchtwanger about a hundred years ago. Wouldn't it be more fun to sit down in a restaurant and ask the waiter for a couple of feuchtwangers, all dressed?

But I digress. Split your baguette. Layer in the mustard, add the sausage, slap on the chili and some raw onions. Open a beer. Turn on the TV. You might get lucky.

Farewell, My Lovely (dir. Dick Richards, 1975) starred Robert Mitchum as the private eye Philip Marlowe. It was also filmed as *Murder, My Sweet* (dir. Edward Dmytryck 1944.) Rent one, rent them both. Contrast and compare thugs.

Wear your yellow shirt, the one that hides the mustard stains. Yeah, you can wear a shirt like that. When you eat by yourself, you can wear what you want. If your chili dog's too messy, tuck a napkin in your collar. Take big bites so all the juices run together. The onions cut into the chili, the mustard brings up the sausage. Heaven is the combination.

Chandler's thug "looked as inconspicuous as a tarantula on a slice of angel food cake." That's what you want for dessert. Angel food cake. Washed down with the last of your beer. Cake and beer don't mix? Says who?

Yeah, and I put my elbows on the table when I want. Moose Molloy did. Nobody was big enough to tell him what to do. Nobody tells me what to do, either. Not when I've got a chili dog, fully-loaded, in my hand.

Red Beans and Rice

Canadians take half-steps in winter. We're prisoners hobbled by chains of ice. But give us a hint of an early spring—a melted snowbank here, a patch of bare sidewalk there—and we kick up our heels as if we'd been given time off for good behaviour.

Like cons on parole, we'll trade rash promises for the merest whiff of freedom. Next year, we'll buy a decent snow shovel. Next year we'll get a pair of ugly boots to keep us warm. Next year, we'll get that hat.

For now, we're content to push our luck, to sit on a chilly chair taking a first glass of outdoor beer with our jackets undone, our cheeks turned to the sun, our dreams as soft as the new green sleeping in the branches of the trees.

Soon it will be so hot there'll be nothing for us but cold shrimp, a leaf of tender lettuce, and a glass of wine cut with sparkling water.

Not so fast. Permit me the heresy of a backward look. There's still a little time for a pot of something that cooks all day, fills your house with warmth and greets you with good smells when you come home at the end of the day.

I'm talking about red beans and rice. This way, please.

Soak a pound of kidney beans in water tonight. Tomorrow morning, sauté a couple of slices of smoked bacon in a big black cast iron pot. If you don't have a big black cast iron pot, improvise. But you really ought to have one.

Cut up three onions, three stalks of celery with their leaves, and three cloves of garlic. Add them to the kettle. Stir them around for a couple of minutes. Add plenty of black pepper and then some more. Add half a teaspoon of cayenne, a teaspoon of thyme and a pair of bay leaves. Add the beans and their soaking liquid.

Now listen. I don't want to be doctrinaire, but I use a couple of smoked pork hocks. You could use a ham bone with plenty of meat on it, but frankly, when there's a ham bone handy, you ought to make bean soup. So get the hocks. You can have the butcher split them if you wish. I like to leave them whole.

Cover everything with two inches of water. Bring to a boil on top of the stove. Cut the heat, put the lid on, stick the pot in the oven at 275°F, and go away for three or four hours.

Wear something light. Leave your sweater in the drawer. You want what's left of the cold to reach your bones. Supper's going to warm you nicely.

There used to be ice beneath your feet. Yesterday, not today. Consider that only the ephemeral has lasting value. Remember the missionary who tried to convert the Greenlanders. He painted the flames of damnation and told terrible stories of the heat of eternal hellfire. The Greenlanders thought about that, talked among themselves, and said they wanted to go there.

Let the day pass pleasantly. Return to the oven and look at what you've done. If you think the beans have thickened up too much, add a little more water. Strip the meat from the hocks, discard the bones and put the meat back in the pot.

Make some white rice. Put a serving of rice in a soup plate, and smother it with a ladle or two of red beans. Garnish with some chopped raw onion, a jolt of hot sauce, and a little splash of vinegar. Open a beer. Give thanks. Summer is icummen in.

Save the leftovers in the freezer for a day in June, to use as a side with your first barbecued ribs. Be grateful for *les neiges d'antan,* without which there is precious little all-day cooking.

WILD MINT

To hell with winter. This is what I'm thinking while I wait for the ice to thaw:

On the way to the creek in the summer, we often frightened snakes. They made a dry sound in the grass. I hate snakes and I hate the sound they make. I was always careful where I stepped.

We smelled of sweat and citronella, and the air was hot and stank of muck. In some places, the bush was thick enough to scratch our faces as we walked, but the water was cold and the pools were full of trout, and there were flowers growing on the banks. The creek was nameless on the maps. You couldn't see it from the road. You had to know where to look.

The Secret Spot.

We caught fish there for years, and gutted them on the bank near a little wooden bridge. When the fish were clean we wrapped them in grass to keep them cool on the way to town. We left the guts for the foxes.

When we got home I always threw the slimy grass against the side of the house, behind the ferns and snapdragons. There was a payoff to my laziness—one spring my mother noticed wild mint in among the flowers. I must have brought it with me from the creek.

The mint flourished there until it threatened to take over everything, but we cut it back hard and it found its size, and every year my mother made jelly when the mint was at its peak.

Mint tastes like spring to me, no matter the time of year. If I visit the folks in the summer, I always head out the back door to take some mint and crush it in my hand and breathe the smell, and then chew on the leaves. If there's any mint jelly in the cupboard, I slip a jar in my suitcase when the visit's over.

Eventually the creek was dammed by beaver, and the water got sluggish and muddy, and the pools were fished to death by other people, friends of friends we shared the secret with.

But the mint still grows behind the house. And if my old man doesn't go fishing any more, my brother occasionally brings him some trout and my mother fries them up and everybody's happy. I could use a bit of that these days.

I have a friend who dreams of fish in winter, when the snow is still on the ground. It's a sign that spring is on the way. After the dream, he goes down into his basement and cleans his tackle box, and strips the old line from his fishing reels and waits.

When I lived there, he'd call me after he'd had the dream. I'd go over for a drink. He'd take his maps and lay them on the table. We'd point to places we'd caught fish. The ones that got away were always five pounds bigger after drinks.

I'm not nuts about drinking near the water, but once I went fishing with a friend who brought a mickey with him in his vest. We took a drink whenever we waded across the stream. And when we were pleasantly drunk, he caught a trout.

I saw him, waist-deep in the water, stripping the fish of its eggs. He swallowed two bright orange strings of them, and chased the eggs with a slug of scotch and crossed the stream again. Roe v. Wade. It made me gag. I didn't do the same when I caught mine.

I moved away from there long ago, and I put my maps in a box. I've moved so much, I'm not sure where the box is anymore. But the way the weather's been, I need to dream of fish. I want to look at maps and find a Secret Spot, and I crave the smell of mint and the taste of speckled trout in butter.

For the moment, all I can do is raise the thermostat and take a glass of something amber, and wait for the ice to thaw.

HE SAID A MOUTHFUL

These days I've been walking to work. I share my route with hip-hop hairdressers who chew gum for breakfast. With minor functionaries. With old men recovering from operations. And, in this neighbourhood, with the insecure and overly-secure of every conceivable gender.

My walk is a brisk forty minutes. Most days, near the half-way point, I pass an old man sitting on his porch. We've developed a relationship of sorts. I wave hello to him. He calls me "Garçon," claps a hand to his mouth and blows me a kiss. This is not something I'm used to, but I find I miss it when he's not there.

His passing parade is me. Mine is different. One morning at twenty past eight I passed a man wearing pajamas. He was eating a sugar bun and high-stepping down the sidewalk as if he were climbing a staircase, trying to squash a butterfly that was always one step up.

He was old and wispy enough to be angelic. His black loafers were so small his bare heels spilled out the back, which may have explained the walk. He hailed a police cruiser at the corner of the street. I hoped he was looking for shoes that fit. I hoped the cops would buy him a decent breakfast, deliver him back to his room, and blow him a kiss goodbye.

This walk is the most exercise I've had in a while. I've been making and taking my lunch. A good one. A sandwich off the roast, some olives, a pair of cookies, two pieces of fruit. And lots of water. Over the course of the week, it's far cheaper than a restaurant and better than the cafeteria downstairs.

Since the walk is almost an hour and a half both ways, it's also food as fuel.

Yes, food as fuel. Here's what I mean. I worked in a paper mill one year. On the sorting tables, with a picaroon. Hauling logs off a conveyor belt as they tumbled out of the barking drums. The sound was deafening, the work was hard, the smell of rotted bark was everywhere. Lunch was all the home-made, high-powered food I could pack in my pail, to give me the strength to get my job done.

The noise and the stench of the mill were invasive. The taste of the food was the only private sensation available. We worked so hard that food took on additional, and more intimate importance. One night on midnight shift a tall, skinny man slammed down his sandwich and said to no one in particular, "How does she expect me to fuck on bologna?" There was a lull in the conversation, and a sadness at the table. Nobody answered. But nobody offered him a better sandwich.

During the silence, a fat man who rarely spoke saw an opportunity. His chance to start and end a conversation, to say something so penetrating we'd forget he was as tongue-tied and confused as the rest of us.

He cleared his throat loudly enough to cut through the din of the mill. He swept us with a gaze and spoke with authority, definitively and for all time. "The woman is the fig. The man is the banana."

He smiled to himself the way an academic does upon the delivery of a *bon mot* at a faculty meeting. We looked at him, open-mouthed. Nobody knew what he meant, or cared. The skinny man went back to his bologna.

CARNIVAL OF CARNIVORES

He had slick hair and dark eyes, the small man in the tired black suit. The woman with him was tall and hard and skinny, with long red nails she didn't use for typing. They walked into Schwartz's like bank robbers. Hungry for each other, I thought. Or maybe just him for her. It was high noon on a Friday.

I was having the usual, a regular smoked meat with fries and a black cherry soda. They took the seats at the end of the table. She sat stiffly and crossed her legs. No nylons. A guy notices these details.

The little man put his elbows on the table, leaned forward and whispered something quickly, softly to the woman. She didn't say a word, she didn't look at him. She looked around the room. But she heard what he said and she nodded.

The waiter came to discuss the menu, but there was no discussion. The little man knew what he wanted. The woman lit a smoke and fidgeted. When the little man looked at me, I smiled. I wanted to be sociable. His eyes were flat. The message was clear: mind your own business. I did.

When the woman was halfway through her cigarette, food started coming in waves. There was a large platter of regular smoked meat, with the bread on the side. A grilled steak, half a spiced chicken, and a couple of franks. A smoked meat on rye. Some grilled liver, and couple of slices of veal.

The man took the sandwich and the fries.

The rest of the food was for her.

She parked her ultra-slim in the ashtray, took a deep breath and let it out with an all-in-a-day's-work sigh. She asked me for the

47

ketchup. I gave it up without a word. I wasn't going to interfere with the little man's play. He didn't touch his sandwich. He wanted to watch her eat. That's what he was hungry for. She didn't disappoint.

She cut into her bloody steak and followed bites of it with bites of mustard-covered sausage. She salted her chicken and ate it with both hands. She laid strip after strip of smoked meat on her plate, swirled it in puddles of mustard and ketchup, and forked it into her mouth. The cigarette died slowly while she ate.

Schwartz's at lunch is always filled with cocky men whose badly fitting Boss suits are going shiny in the recession. They sit cheek-by-jowl with tattooed punks and whole tables of fat guys who spill out of baseball jackets and who order their smoked meat lean. Circulating among them are half a dozen elderly waiters with bald heads and white shirts, with pink faces and soft hands. Everyone stared at the woman.

The room was hushed. All of us wanted to sit where the little man sat. We wanted her to look at us the way she looked at her meat.

When she was done, she pushed her plate away and wiped her hands. She checked her lipstick with a pocket mirror and took a fresh cigarette. He lit it, but she didn't look at him. This was the ritual, a part of the game.

The waiter came and cleared the plates, smiled at her and left the bill. The little man with the slick hair studied the slip of paper. He double-checked the addition, and called the waiter back. The waiter had left some meat off the bill. It was an easy mistake. There'd been so much of it. The little man wanted to pay for everything he ordered. The woman stubbed her cigarette. Her nails shone redder than before.

They got up. She wore a grey skirt that hung loosely, as on a clothesline. You could see the bones of her hips when she moved. The sweater she wore was threadbare and clean. Her eyes were dull, as if she'd seen too much and none of it had impressed. She was anxious to leave.

Every man in Schwartz's wanted to leave with her.

BRUNSWICK STEW

I like to count the squirrels in the park. I don't mark out grids, take a random sample and multiply that number by the square root of dogs running loose after them. I'm no wildlife biologist. I just like to know how many there are. Last week, during a five minute stroll on the way home from work, I counted forty-seven. This is my personal best.

If you want to measure yourself against that mark, start at the south end of Parc LaFontaine and walk up the east side of the pond, as far as the statue of that old bushwhacker, Dollard des Ormeaux. And if you see the legendary Albino Squirrel of Parc LaFontaine, let me know.

Squirrel is Greek, derived from *skia*, "shadow" and *ouros*, "tail." How apt. Two of my tally lost their tails to the snapping jaws of dogs. They looked mildly embarrassed by the lack of a nether appendage, but embarrassment beats death any day of the week, and with their little hands folded in front of their chests, they seemed glad that dogs are stupid.

During my formative years, I identified closely with the protagonist of Beatrix Potter's *The Tale of Squirrel Nutkin*. I confided this to no one. The world is a cruel place, which lesson I learned in the company of so-called friends when, overcome with the emotion of a Saturday afternoon at the movies, I leapt from my seat and cried "Run, Bambi, run!" No way was I adding "Squirrel" to the taunts.

Over time, I outgrew the sting of that. My taste in literature, friends and movies matured. Still, I was troubled when I read that Davy Crockett would frequently shoulder Old Betsy and knock off a Nutkin or two for lunch.

Davy would go nuts in the park at this time of year. The squirrels I see are fat, their coats thick and shiny. They look good enough to eat, and I'm surprised more people don't try a plateful. Squirrels are not endangered. There is no shortage of them here. Herd management is not a problem. Utter a brisk "tsk-tsk-tsk" and see how quickly they come running.

Those of us trained in the ways of the woods know how to trap them humanely. You simply prop one end of a box on a stick, to which you've tied a length of string. Put stale bread beneath the box. When the squirrel approaches the bait, a tug of the string drops the box, and presto! You have the principal ingredient for Brunswick Stew, that staple of the bush camp and the hobo village.

You will need six adult squirrels, cut up and browned in bacon fat in a Dutch oven. Add a carrot, an onion and a rib of celery, all finely chopped. Add a couple of quarts of water, bring to a boil and simmer until the meat falls off the bone. Remove the vegetables and discard. Then remove the squirrel from the broth, strip the meat from the bones, discard the bones and put the meat back in the pot.

Add two slices of diced smoked bacon. Add a quarter teaspoon of cayenne, and salt and pepper to taste. Add a cup of chopped onion, half a dozen chopped tomatoes, four medium potatoes, some fresh thyme, a bay leaf and some parsley.

Simmer for another hour. Purists add two cups of lima beans and cook until they're tender. I hate lima beans. Some people throw in a couple of cups of okra to thicken things up. If you don't want okra, thicken your stew with a *roux*.

Add two cups of corn just before you finish cooking. Variously you can add hot sauce to taste, and a teaspoon or so of Worcestershire. If you plan to eat this while you're listening to the Neville Brothers, throw in a bit of gumbo filé powder.

This recipe represents years of development and regional variation. The original recipe for Brunswick stew is much more simple. Brown some bacon in a stew pot, add some onion, add your squirrel and brown that, and then cover with water and simmer slowly until the whole thing turns to mush. Ditch the bones, season with salt and pepper, and thicken with stale bread or crackers.

You may substitute rabbit if you haven't the heart to trap a Nutkin. If, when you think of rabbit, you think of Peter, chicken works just as well.

WASKAGANISH

The Dash-8 dashes north from Montreal to Chibougamau and Nemiscau, and then heads west to the James Bay delta. The Grand Council of the Crees is meeting in Waskaganish. That's Fort Rupert on your old map.

I'm working with a group of Cree journalists. We're there to produce three live radio broadcasts from the gym where the meetings will be held.

The town is crowded with delegates, and there aren't many places for outsiders to stay. No one has the luxury of a single room. Everyone doubles up.

The new lodge where we stay has the scope of a cathedral. Its floor-to-ceiling windows overlook the Rupert River. In the middle of the dining room there is a giant stone fireplace which won't draw smoke, so there's never a fire burning there, and the room is always cold.

But the weather softens with our arrival, and Waskaganish turns muddy quickly. Management is nervous about the carpets. They make us take our boots off at the entrance, and for three days the lodge is full of big guys in parkas who tippy-toe across the floors in their stocking feet. They grin at each other as if they were new kids in kindergarten. As if their moms were watching.

We have breakfast at sun-up. I warm my hands on a cup of coffee. The clouds are goose-feather grey, with streaks of pink bleeding through. I eat steam-table eggs with sausage and bacon and toast. I stare out the window. You are what you eat, you are where you eat.

The horizon is an inch of trees against the far shore. Someone drives a half-ton down to the dock. I see him unload a can of gas, a grub box and some supplies. He pushes his canoe across a crust of ice, starts the kicker and heads downstream to his traps.

He does all this without a second thought, as easily as you or I walk to the bus stop. He's done it hundreds of times. You can't tell him one good reason why his trap-line should be flooded. And that, as it turns out, is a fair summary of the content of the meetings—to hell with Hydro Quebec.

The Grand Council proceeds carefully. The Cree speak from the heart about whatever they want, no matter how close they are to the agenda, and everyone listens carefully when an elder has something to say. No one bangs the table and calls out "Point of order!"

We work from morning to midnight preparing our daily broadcast. We grab fast food when we can from Jacob's, a smoke-filled joint near the school. Hamburger steaks, poutine, club sandwiches. We miss as many meals as we eat.

Everything here is done with cash. There's no bank in town, there are no money machines, and there's no way to use a credit card. If you live in Waskaganish, the general store takes your cheque on deposit, and you spend against your credit. The closest bank is a plane ride away in Val d'Or.

Waskaganish is a strongly Pentecostal community, but not everyone is convinced. One evening I see a man standing on the steps of the church. He holds the door open and looks in. The light from the church is yellow and spills against his jacket. I can hear angry, cadenced preaching. But Cree is a soft language and the shouting sounds wrong, somehow. The man at the door doesn't move.

The conference ends with a community feast. Everyone sits at long tables piled high with plates of caribou, roast goose, and moose nose. There are pots of tea and plates of boudin, a kind of sweet bannock with molasses and raisins. You are what you eat. They're Cree.

Later that night, as we tip-toe to our room at two a.m., I notice a young man sitting by himself in a small room off the lobby of the hotel. His head is bent, and he's intent on something I can't see. I'm curious about what he's doing. He has a plastic bag full of tamarack twigs, and a roll of cord. He's making a little goose decoy, the kind you see in gift shops. The room is full of the fragrance of the tamarack, and the smell of his cigarette. He smiles at us.

I ask him how he manages to shape the body of the goose so perfectly. He says he sometimes uses a styrofoam ball. That's progress. In the old days, they used to use a ball of twigs.

He tells me that if the little souvenir decoy loses its smell of tamarack, all you have to do is splash some water on it and the smell will come back as rich as before. The next day, I buy a small twig goose at the gift shop.

On the way home, the plane picks up a group of skinny, nervous men who've been building the Route du Nord. Unlike the Cree, they're twitchy after three months in the bush. Their eyes dart everywhere. They talk too loud.

Perhaps they have reason to be on edge. The road they're building will bring the Cree more harm than good, in the form of pulp trucks, hunters from the south, and surveyors from Hydro Quebec.

The road builders, if they know this, may not care.

They're eating salted nuts. At eleven a.m., you are not only what you eat, you are also what you drink. They call for doubles from the bar cart.

They're bushed.

The Feathered Vegetable

We boil their eggs, we roast their flesh, we crack their bones. We even call each other "chicken" when we want to hurl an insult. We ought to mean that as a compliment, given what the chicken does for us.

Carnivores are ingrates, I suppose.

My father, bless his heart, won't eat one. This has something to do with the Great Depression, his mother, and a henhouse full of pet-victims clucking in the back yard. That's good enough for me; everyone has quirks, and if choice is freely taken anywhere, it ought to be at the table.

But I think he's carried it a bit too far. His Depression was sixty years ago. Even in my family, that's a long time to hold a grudge. Lately, in the manner of fathers and sons, I've taken to disputing that his Depression was any worse than mine is now. He doesn't argue this one very hard.

I don't have a henhouse, but sometimes I wish I did. Not only for the meat, but for the eggs as well; world-wide, there are around 400 billion eggs produced every year, by nearly 4 billion chickens, most of whom spend their entire lives in indoor cages. This is cruel and inexcusable. I say we ought to be allowed to raise them freely, at home in our back yards, or in the communal laneways of our towns.

And why not? Henry IV of France raised his own chickens a thousand years ago. Call him the Barnyard Monarch. We might not have to wait as long for the next one. No, not Elizabeth R. The Prince of Wales is standing in the wings.

No other food is so versatile. There are so-called vegetarians who take a little chicken now and then, on the theory that the chicken is nothing more than a vegetable with feathers.

They could be right. The fact is, we've been eating a lot of chicken in this house lately. Wings bought in bulk for $2.75 a kilo, broiled and dressed with lemon and garlic and *herbes de Provençe*. Stewing hens made into soups and boiled dinners. *Poulet au grain,* when I can afford one, cut up and fried. Often, if I'm frying one, I'll save the breasts for later. Then, I'll grill them and serve them with a sauce made from a reduction of orange juice and chicken broth.

If you're tired of chicken in this new Depression, here's something that will make your tired old bird taste new. If you don't have all the ingredients, borrow what you need from your friends and feed them.

Stuff a chicken with four ounces of pancetta. And a dozen fresh leaves of sage. Also ten juniper berries. And a bay leaf. Two teaspoons of rosemary (fresh, or dried and blanched in boiling water.) And half a dozen peppercorns. No substitutes for any of this, please.

Stick everything in the cavity and truss the bird tightly with string. Salt and pepper the outside of the chicken, and put it in a roasting pan with a quarter-cup of olive oil. Roast it for an hour and a quarter at 400°F, and turn it every fifteen minutes.

You read me right. At 400°F, this is not your mother's chicken. Nor my mother's, given my old man's attitude. This is Chicken in the Manner of a Suckling Pig. *C'est cochon comme ça.*

This recipe is adapted from Giuliano Bugialli's *The Fine Art of Italian Cooking.* The book is worth every penny to own. Do this chicken my way, or get the book and do it his. Do it as you will. This is a dish which, when you eat it, will make you raise your eyebrows in wonder and thanksgiving.

Serve with your best mashed potatoes and a good green salad. As you eat, think of a red wheel barrow, glazed with rain water, beside the white chickens. One of them might have been this one.

MUSEUM FOOD

A load of turbot spills across the table. Their mouths are frozen open and their eyes are blank. Sea creatures have no dignity on land.

A woman approaches with a reed basket. She lifts a fish and sniffs a gill. She wrinkles up her nose. The fishmonger looks at her. Eels in buckets splash his feet, and giant salmon hang from iron hooks behind him. At the edge of the frame, someone stands in the half-light, watching and sharpening a knife. It's been a long day. The customer is always right.

In the shop next door, two dead white ducks and a pheasant lie beside each other on a wooden chopping block. Their necks are limp, still warm. Someone's left a glass of wine on the block beside a cleaver, a whetstone and a plate with a crust of bread. The light is softest where it falls on the pheasant's feathers. Everybody's got to eat.

You move along. See those apples? No one grows that variety any more, and these are not for sale, but you can smell them if you close your eyes.

They're at the Montreal Museum of Fine Arts, in paintings on the walls. We own them, and we ought not to have to pay a lot of money to look at them. Go at six o'clock on Wednesday evenings, when admission is half-price.

Put yourself in the picture. Find a Last Supper and pretend you're an apostle. Put your elbows on the table and imagine saying "Jesus, pass the butter."

Now look at some paintings from 17th-century France. Imagine living in those days. You could pick up a drumstick and point with it then. You could wipe your greasy hands on the back of the restaurant's dog. You could drink a glass of wine and gossip in whispers about Cardinal Richelieu.

What's Richelieu cooking up with the king? "If God forbade drinking, would He have made wine so good?" That's what Richelieu said. Yeah, and if God had been any kind of democrat, He would have made the good stuff less expensive.

Okay. You see that basket of peaches in the painting over there? Stare at it. Remember the first time you put a peach in red wine and ate it? If you've never done it that way with a peach, now's the time.

Watch your step on the way out. Moishe Safdie, the famous hot-shot architect, has made us Montrealers look like boobs descending a staircase. The stairs in the MMFA are built with long treads and short risers. They are impossible to walk on. They are built for no known stride. They have more to do with Safdie's arrogance than they have to do with the length of anybody's legs.

To hell with him.

Get a loaf of bread and some grapes on your way home. You want an orange or two, and a couple of pears—Boscs because of their beauty, and because their skin is brown as deerhide. Buy one with a leaf still on the stem.

At home, drape a white cloth on your dinner table. Use a sheet if you have to. Wash the wax off the apples. Rinse the grapes. Take out your best plate and put the fruit on it. Break your bread in pieces and scatter it artfully. Don't worry about the crumbs. Leave them where they fall.

Lay out some cheese. Pour a glass of wine. Kill the lights, light the candles. Stand back and look at what you've done. To hell with Safdie; anyone's steps are better than his. And to hell with Richelieu, while we're at it. Painting is better than politics, and you've just made a painting you can eat.

A Taste of Spring in Winter

Every spring my father used to send me out to the back yard for the annual harvest of the dandelion greens. I went against my will, armed with a kitchen knife and a plastic bag. I was embarrassed to be out there on my hands and knees—you know how kids are—and I punished the lawn with my dangerous knife. If dandelions were such a hot treat, I wondered, why doesn't he pick them himself?

It was worse when the neighbour watched me work. He sprayed his lawn with weed-killer, and trimmed it like it was a putting green. He glared at me as if we raised our dandelions to spite him. Maybe we did. You know how neighbours are.

Those dandelions died a terrible death. They were too bitter for me, and I made them pay for it. Now that I'm more mature and have fewer taste buds to work with, I'll eat them whenever I can. They remind me of spring.

That's not out of place these last few days of winter. Mind you, the air is getting soft, and if I've shaved particularly close and the sun's shining and I'm standing out of the wind, I can almost imagine spring on my cheek. But I have to close my eyes to do it.

I had a salad at a friend's the other night that brought back thoughts of spring and my old man. Composed of radicchio, some marinated goat cheese, butter lettuce and some dandelion greens, it was dressed in a vinaigrette, and it didn't make a damn bit of difference that the snow was falling outside. One forkful and there I was, kneeling on the lawn again, stabbing dandelions and cursing my old man. I hadn't thought of that in years. It felt good. We do whatever it takes to make it through to spring.

Dandelions are not always available. For a more reliable mid-winter pick-me-up, I rely on pesto. Made with two cups of tightly-packed basil. Half a cup of good olive oil. A couple of tablespoons of pine nuts and two or three or four cloves of garlic, a quarter-cup of grated romano and half a cup of grated parmigiano-reggiano. Add two tablespoons of butter, if you can afford the calories—I often leave the butter out. Throw in a bit of salt. Chop, grind or process the basil, oil and nuts, then beat in the cheeses and the butter by hand.

Pesto freezes very well, although if you do that, you should remember to omit the cheese and add it fresh when you've thawed it out. Don't trust anyone who says you can make it with walnuts or with parsley. Or any other kinds of cheese, or with any nouvelle-whacko ingredients.

Last year we bought a bushel of fresh basil at the Jean Talon Market. We made eighteen jars of pesto. That gave us a jar a week to take care of winter's worst. We still have a few jars in the freezer. They are emerald sentinels standing shoulder to shoulder against the darkness of winter. We ration them carefully. They are reminders of warmer days. Sometimes you have to look behind to see ahead.

I rely on the freezer a lot. My old man bought it for me as a present when I left to work in the Arctic. He thought that was a good joke, sending a freezer to the frozen north. It was no joke. The first two years I was in Iqaluit, fresh food came in only once a week by plane—depending on the weather. I used the freezer to keep a supply of the basics on hand at all times.

Unfortunately, a freezer isn't always foolproof. Once in Regina, a real estate person came to appraise our house. She unwittingly turned off the wrong switch when she came up from the basement. We went on holidays the next day and came back to discover six quarts of rotting Northern Ontario blueberries, several warm jars of beef and chicken broth, some mouldy strawberry pies, various unidentifiable packages—I don't always label as well as I should—and eleven jars of pesto gone woefully wrong.

Ah, well. Buy basil fresh whenever you see it. Make pesto whenever you're fed up with February or real estate agents. Pretend you're in Genoa and the cold is just some freakish aberration.

If you see dandelion greens, get them too. Try the greens with olive oil and lemon juice, some salt and fresh pepper. If you can't find dandelions, get some radicchio. Make your salad with that, some toasted almonds and a decent pear.

Make sure you've got good bread on the table. You'll want to clean the summer off your plate. Oh, and listen to Giuseppe Verdi while you eat.

You know. Joe Greens.

A Plate of Spaghetti

Today you're going to eat, drink, sing, read—and act—Italian. I want you to start by going to the film store to rent Fellini's *Nights of Cabiria*. Italy was being born out of the ashes of the Second World War when that movie was being made. It's as good a place as any to begin.

Now go to the liquor store and get a decent bottle of wine. It doesn't have to be chianti, but it has to be Italian. Use your imagination. Italians do. All those wines, all that pasta.

Head up the street for a tin of plum tomatoes, a bottle of the best olive oil you can find, and a little fresh basil. Whistle "O Sole Mio" while you're walking to the store. You know the tune. Think of Elvis Presley, singing "It's Now or Never." You're going to make a fine Italian. If you get stopped by the cops on the way to the market, tell them you're a legitimate businessman.

Walk with confidence, walk without a care. While you're whistling, look around. Think of Here as There. Consider what will happen if and when Italy separates into south and north, and pray that it doesn't upset Canadian-Italian trade relationships. We send them durum wheat, they send us rigatoni, bucatini, orecchiette. We get the better deal.

Pay for your groceries and head for home. On the way, you might stop at the book store. See if you can find *Among Women Only* by Cesare Pavese.

And you want opera. The concert at Caracalla is okay. Pavarotti's on a diet. Isn't that a shame? He isn't going to eat as well as you tonight. He'd better not.

62

Now that you're home, pour a glass of wine and start to cook. Put some olive oil in a pan. Sliver three or four cloves of garlic as thinly as you can and add them to the oil. When the perfume of the garlic rises, you start to sing.

Drain the tomatoes and add them to the pan. Grind some fresh pepper, add a teaspoon of salt and simmer twenty minutes. This is so simple.

If you want pasta arrabbiata, add half a teaspoon of pepper flakes and simmer a little longer. If you want to be complicated, toss in a piece of chicken you've browned beforehand, and let it finish cooking in the sauce.

Consider that there are almost as many different shapes for pasta as there are states of the Italian mind. There are bridegrooms, butterflies and shells; there are quills and sparrows' tongues; there are little moustaches and priests' hats. Frankly, if Italy had spent less time inventing new shapes for pasta and more time on good government, we'd still have a Holy Roman Empire.

You have to love a people who'd rather eat than rule, but while we're on the subject of government, don't be fooled by those pejoratives about the so-called Italian Parliament. Italy has had more national elections than any other country in the world since the end of WW II, not because we're bad at government, but because we're good at compromise and coalition.

Where was I? Oh, yes. Tonight you want to dine classically. Add a handful of spaghetti to a pot of boiling water. How much spaghetti? As much as you can circle between your thumb and forefinger will do for one. How long to cook? Read the directions on the package.

When the spaghetti's ready, drain it and toss it with the sauce. Dress it with the fresh basil and serve it up in a soup plate. Don't twirl your spaghetti with the help of a spoon. Learn to twirl it with your fork and nothing else, the way the Italians do.

After supper, have another glass of wine. Watch the movie, mindful that poverty humiliates; it produces anger and then numbness. Finally, it almost always produces the artistry of hope. Fellini said "All art is autobiographical—the pearl is the oyster's autobiography." *Nights of Cabiria* is a chapter of hope in the autobiography of Fellini.

Now read the opening sentence of the Pavese. "I arrived in Turin with the last January snow just like a juggler or a nougat peddler." You will dream of pearls the colour of nougat tonight.

Whisper the last words of Puccini's "Nessun Dorma" as you fall asleep...*all'alba vincero*. At dawn, I will win. And you will. You'll have leftovers. Spaghetti arrabbiata is wonderful for breakfast.

A BOWL OF RED

Chili is the perfect NAFTA food. It was invented in the USA with Mexican ingredients and it throws enough heat to keep a Canadian warm in the winter. It's also cheap, which is an important consideration now that so few of us have jobs.

But no one makes chili any more. You hardly ever see it on a restaurant menu, and the only time you see it on TV is during the first ten seconds of some antacid commercial. I hate that. Spicy food doesn't cause heartburn, bad cooking does.

If you want chili, you have to make it at home. There are two schools of thought on how to proceed. The main one you're familiar with. Brown some meat, add some onions and green peppers, some tomatoes, beans, cumin and chili powder. This is the usual way.

There is another way, recommended by chili-Jesuits who make their chili with meat and chilis, and nothing else. The meat is beef, browned in its own fat. The seasoning is a mix of dried and powdered chilis. There are no tomatoes added. Beans, if you want 'em, are on the side. I've made it both ways. I like it both ways.

I do have some advice.

Don't use hamburger. Don't pay for someone else to cut your meat. Don't pay for fat and water. Buy the toughest-looking lump of beef you can find. It'll be cheaper than hamburger and it will taste better. Cut it up yourself; cubes if you prefer, or strips, which is how I like it. You think that kind of meat's too tough? Come on. Chili melts the hardest hearts, slow cooking softens the toughest beef.

Also, if you're going to use beans, use real beans. Canned ones are mushy, they cost ten times what dry beans cost and they don't taste as good. Be a cowperson and try pinto beans. Or be trendy and use black beans. You can even mix things up—use a combination of red kidney beans and white cannellini beans. Just remember to soak them overnight, and to cook them before you add them to your pot of chili.

Secret ingredients? Some people add beer or mustard to a pot of chili. Some people even add celery salt, although I've no idea why. Chili's not a subtle dish, with a dash of this, a splash of that, and a tiny bit of something else.

However (you knew there'd be a however!), if you see any of those dried ancho chilis, the ones that are dusty and black and look like chunks of bakelite plastic after a nuclear meltdown, buy them. Take one and crumble it up. Pour boiling water over it and let it steep for a bit while you're browning the meat. Throw the ancho chili and a cup of the soaking liquid into the pot. However you make your chili, adding an ancho will improve it. Anchos are ineffably smoky, with a taste as complex as good chocolate.

Serve your chili plain, or with some raw chopped onion or a little grated cheddar on top. No sour cream. That would be effete.

I like a bowl of chili once a month, but for some reason the smell of it makes me sad. The last time I made some, we went out while the pot simmered and when we came back the house was warm and filled with the smell of chili and meat and beans. I thought my heart was breaking. And I've no idea why. I'm not sure I want to know. But I will say this. When you make chili, make a big pot. You want leftovers. Chili, like a broken heart, improves with age.

CHEW ON THIS

Statistics show that for every ten fillings drilled and packed by dentists, one will be extracted by a piece of toffee. Eight of every ten fillings yanked by toffee come from fillings in the back teeth of toffee-chewers who are too stupid to have learned their lesson the first time.

You're smart. You gave up chewing toffee long ago, although you will, on occasion, suck on a piece and pray.

You have teeth that seize up in the cold. You have other teeth that don't feel right, although you can't say how. And you have a pair on one side of your mouth you gave up using long ago because they can't take the pressure of a direct bite. When you dine with others, you hope no one notices the contortions you go through, shifting mouthfuls leeward.

The adjective "toothsome" makes you flinch. How the hell are you supposed to chew thirty-two times when each bite produces a twinge. You want your teeth marked, like faucets, with letters to indicate hot or cold.

Your dentist has no answers. He no longer uses a treadle-powered drill, and he is a marginally better person than the one played by Laurence Olivier in *The Boys From Brazil*. Still, the last time you sat in his chair, you got up drooling with a lop-sided grin and a mouth that wouldn't close properly. But you walked with a spring in your step, because under local anaesthetic, those new-age tapes were strangely tuneful and compelling. And because your wallet was five hundred dollars lighter.

It was worth it, if only for the week immediately following that visit, when you ate with confidence. It was worth it if your dentist gave you nitrous oxide. That's laughing gas to you. Ask your dentist all about it. It's perfectly legal and plenty of fun.

In the old days, everyone had strong teeth. In *Domestic Manners of the Americans*, Frances Trollope (1780–1863) reported seeing a group of Yankee soldiers cleaning their teeth with their pocket knives. Nobody does that any more.

Perhaps it was Mrs. Trollope who, when dining with the general, asked "You mean to say water never touches your lips? Pray, then, what do you use to brush your teeth?" He replied "A light sauternes, madam."

My grandfather died before I was born. His choppers were magnificent, according to family legend. He is supposed to have used his teeth to pull a four-inch nail out of a piece of wood. The nail had been driven down to within a quarter inch of the head.

I never believed this story myself.

Then I got a job working as a labourer. On my first day of work, an old man sitting on the end of the bench looked up when the foreman called my name. "I knew your grandfather," he said. "Tough bugger. He could pull nails out of boards with his teeth." He spat. He looked at me and grinned. His teeth were false.

Mine are soft and gapped, an endless source of worry. Here's the point. Some of us have no dental insurance plan. Spare ribs and gazpacho hurt.

The ability to enjoy food properly, fearlessly, ought to be enshrined in the Charter of Rights and Freedoms. The health of one's mouth ought not depend on the health of one's wallet.

Here's a question for those wonderful old socialists from Saskatchewan who had their big chance thirty years ago. Why isn't dentistry covered by Medicare? Could it be that Tommy Douglas didn't care for toffee, or for those who eat it?

A MESSAGE TO THE VOTERS

My friends, it's apple blossom time.

This year, I promise to walk beneath the fragrant branches in the morning. When the day begins, I'll look toward the mountains where the dew is drifting upward through the apple trees.

This year, I promise to sit quietly on an applewood bench. When my mind is empty of thought, I'll write apple poems all day long: *Spring night, apple-blossom dawn.* Or, *If I could, I'd sing like apple petals falling.*

I am the only politician in Quebec with the nerve to make these promises.

When I am elected, the Ministry of Verse will institute a contest for apple blossom poems, and books of new ones will be published every year.

As you know, the Japanese do this for cherry blossoms. I am calling for an all-party commission to study the connection between world domination and the adoration of blossoms.

If it works for cherries, I say it ought to work for apples.

When I am elected, my government will give cider-makers in this province the right to make real Québécois calvados, one that burns with a clear blue flame. This has a certain nationalist appeal, *n'est-ce pas?*

If we have to separate, I say we ought to be able to celebrate with something made here in Quebec.

As premier, I will restore some of the tried-and-true superstitions. I'll take immediate action and advise the Minister of Health to send leaflets to every home reminding all Quebeckers that to bring a branch of apple blossoms into the house is to invite sickness.

The Minister Responsible for the Family will tell everyone in the province to get busy, because a good year for apples is a good year for twins.

The Minister Responsible for Singles will advise all unmarried people that if they put the peel of an apple, in a single strip, behind the front door, the first person who enters will bear the Christian name of the unmarried person's future spouse.

My government, in conjunction with the Ministry of Courting, will advise the young to whisper a sweetheart's name at night, then toss an apple pip into the fire, saying "If you love me, pop and fly; if you hate me, lay and die."

Or whatever that is in French.

If I become premier—*when* I become premier—the Ministry of Pork Butchers will be delegated with the responsibility to invent a specific charcuterie based on pork and apples. I want pork loin smoked over apple branches for everyone here at home, and I'll see that we export it abroad to all our Canadian neighbours.

My government will provide special grants to old men on cold nights, so they can afford to heat a cup of cider with a poker taken red-hot from the fire. And if that cider becomes too hot to drink, I will have a special corps of nurses from the Eastern Townships trained to show them how to lower the temperature with a shot of calvados.

We'll all sleep the better for it.

Chers amis, the planks of my platform are made of solid apple wood. None of my opponents dares to say the same.

It's nearly apple blossom time.

Vote for me and I'll make all the fat, bald parish priests rouse themselves to perform Apple Masses on their golden altars. Vote for me and Isaac Newton and Snow White will be our patron saints. Vote for me and every Sunday after Apple Mass, I'll dish out apple pie and call it *tarte aux pommes*.

BOILED DINNER

There were fruit flies in the kitchen the other day. We must have brought them home with us, with the apples from the store. They remind me of the old joke. Waiter, what's that fly doing in my soup? In my case, it wasn't soup.

It was the time of summer jobs, and my buddy Ken and I were going off to work on the highway. When the jobs were over and we'd made pots of money, we were going to buy a car and drive across the country. We were going to be a couple of Kerouacs on the road.

We were sitting in his mother's dining room. We weren't looking at any maps. When you're planning to hit the road and you live in the dead centre of nowhere, in the dead centre of the country, the biggest decision you have to make is east or west.

Something simmered on the stove. I could smell celery and beef, onions and turnips and salt. It smelled like the ocean on a summer day. I asked Ken what it was. He said boiled dinner, although if he'd been Kerouac, he and *memère* would have called it *pot au feu*.

Our house didn't have a dining room. In my house we ate in the kitchen. Ken filled two soup plates, and brought a stack of rye bread and a plate of butter to the dining room table. I grabbed a slice of bread and picked up a spoon and tucked in.

Boiled dinner was new to me. I was used to beef that was braised or stewed and served with gravy. One spoonful of broth and I began to wonder why. It was a revelation.

We ate and added up the money we were going to make. Ken knew a guy with a Zephyr for sale. We figured Jack Kerouac would never have driven a Zephyr, but this one was old and cheap and we knew the guy who was selling it. We figured he wouldn't screw us.

Ken was a fastidious eater who dabbed his lips after every spoonful. I tried not to spill anything on the table cloth. As I split a piece of potato with my spoon, a small drowned fruit fly rose to the surface and came to rest near some parsley. Its little wings were limp and lifeless. Its little legs were dangling in the broth. It was a classic moment.

"What's this doing in my soup?" I grinned.

I should have kept my mouth shut. Ken pushed away his bowl in disgust and took mine away from me.

I asked him to bring me another one. It was only a little fly and the boiled dinner was superb. Besides, the whole point of boiled dinner is that it is boiled; no fruit fly could have harmed it. But what I'd said took the edge off the day and it probably spoiled supper in Ken's house that night.

It also took the edge off planning the trip. We headed for the pool room, where the flies kept to themselves. Not long after that, we started our summer jobs.

There are deer flies and horse flies and black flies and bluebottles in the bush. You don't want them in your dinner, boiled or not, and if there are none on your plate it's because a fastidious cook has removed them.

Summer was long, and the pots of money we made were smaller than we thought. We bought the car anyway. It broke down a week after we got it tuned up and we sold it for a loss. We never hit the road, except to work on it.

As for Ken, the last time we had dinner all I could think about was…oh, hell, I think it was the backstroke.

A ROSE BY ANY OTHER NAME

Raw garlic is so powerful, some prizefighters chew it like candy before they enter the ring. This may have a medicinal effect, as trainers think. It may promote vigour in the ring, the way sexual abstinence is reckoned to do. But no matter which way you slice it, raw garlic on the breath will help repel any opponent in a clinch.

Of course, it also repels vampires. My advice, if you plan to go ten rounds with Dracula, is to wear the stinking rose and chew it, too.

According to garlic legend, when Satan stepped from the garden of Eden after The Fall, onions sprang from where he placed his right hoof, and garlic arose from where he placed his left. In that case, I'd say eating the fruit from the Tree of Knowledge paid off handsomely—where there is no garlic, there is no paradise. And had there been no garlic, there would have been no me.

During the Spanish flu epidemic in 1917, there were deaths in every family on the block. But Nonna kept my grandfather, their dozen children and the boarder healthy with liberal doses of garlic from her garden. My dad was born pink and screaming that year, and I'm here now.

My experience with garlic in bulk also has a Spanish connection. I was almost twenty, and the island of Ibiza was rank, not with flu, but with Canadian painters living in villas on their grants. They howled at the moon with trombones.

Not me. I was living in a rented room with a bed, a chair, a desk for my typewriter, and a sink. The rent was thirty-five bucks a month. This was cheap rent, even on an island of cheap rent, but I was learning how to write, and I wanted my lessons to last as long as possible.

My landlady was an Algerian, so old she looked sun-dried. She liked me because I spoke a bit of French, and because I made my own bed when she gave me two clean sheets on Monday.

She kept to herself, but she had spies. Landladies do, and she always knew when I had a guest stay over. No matter how late we sneaked in and how early we left in the morning, she knew. She'd get that boys-will-be-boys look on her face, and nick me an extra dollar when I paid the rent on the first of the month.

She made a weekly pot of yellow stew with cloves of garlic floating on the top. Hundreds of cloves of garlic, more garlic in that one pot that I'd eaten in my life. And she herself reeked with an assertive, garlicky smell that seemed to arise from her breasts. This may have been because she never took off any of her sweaters, and the smell of garlic ripened on her skin and in her clothes.

I actually loved the smell, and I'd recognize her in an instant if I smelled her now. In fact, we've eaten so much garlic this winter that if I were a synesthete, able to interpret aroma as colour, I could paint her portrait.

We've eaten chicken with forty cloves of garlic. I've roasted garlic cloves in olive oil until they're soft and sweet; I keep them covered with oil in a jar, for use on the weekly pizza. We've baked whole heads of garlic in the oven, and smeared the creamy result on good fresh bread and washed it down with wine.

However, my sweetie got the flu this winter, so garlic may not be as powerful as I once believed. Come to think of it, I've never smelled a trace of garlic in her sweat. Not that I'm complaining, you understand—she has yet to repel me in the clinch.

A Death in the Family

The last time I saw him, he was eighty-seven years old and he was living in an upstairs room in my cousin Mary's house. His wife Josie was long since dead and sadness from that was still in him.

His hearing was bad and he was troubled by cataracts, but he had an old man's eye for detail and he loved to tell a story. My uncle Frank. We sat at the kitchen table, talking and playing casino.

I was in town on a short visit from Montreal. Frank told me he'd lived in Montreal in 1926, not far from where I live now. He worked in a flour mill on the Lachine Canal, and that summer he played baseball for money in Parc LaFontaine. That's just down the street. I told him they still play ball in the park, but not for money any more.

Later in his life he worked as a pilot on the Great Lakes. He told me he once steered a new ship through the locks, not by watching where he was going, but by watching the wake of the ship.

When I asked him why he'd done that, he said it was because the captain was new, it was his first trip down the Seaway, and he was so worried about scraping the sides of the ship against the narrow locks that he stood in front of the window in the wheelhouse and blocked Frank's view. The captain wouldn't move when Frank asked him to. But Frank was an old hand by then. He'd made the trip dozens of times, and he wasn't about to get upset. He simply turned around and kept the ship on course by watching the back end of the ship and steering that.

I told him some of the factories along the canal had been converted into condos. When he lived in Montreal, he'd carried sacks of flour and sweated in the summer heat; now most of the sweating in those converted mills is done on exercycles. The thought of it made Frank laugh.

He poured me a rye and water and smoked a cigarette. He was a strapping man with long arms and strong hands, and a union man's habit of looking you in the eye when he smiled. But he was old and growing smaller and his hands trembled in a way I'd never seen before.

Frank was a man who made no secret of his appetites. He grew apples in his back yard, and crushed them for cider. Some of the cider he distilled, a minor family art and one that's almost disappeared, unless my cousins are keeping something from me.

Sometimes I dropped by his house on weekends when I was a teen. I always knew when he'd been running the still—the whole neighbourhood smelled like baking bread. Frank would say "Here, see what you think of this," as he filled my glass with something ice-cold and innocent, save for the smoke that rose from it. I smiled as I drank, pleased to be asked my opinion.

He and Auntie Josie often ate with my parents. They shared big, hot suppers of rigatoni with tomato sauce, roasts of chicken and pork. Grilled eggplant. Salads of garden lettuce and trays of olives and salami and artichokes in oil.

Sometimes after supper Frank played his mandolin and my dad played banjo while my mother and my auntie Jo cleaned up. Then the four of them would play cards, and I learned friendship listening to their laughter.

Frank would have been ninety this August.

I went home for the funeral last week.

The funeral was quick and quiet. I've been away for a long time. We're a big family and we marry young; some of my cousins have grandchildren whose names I'll never remember.

Things change. After the funeral there wasn't a bottle of wine in sight. Nobody grabbed a glass and stepped down to the basement for a taste of something hard. There was no lasagna and nobody played the mandolin.

I spent a few days at home with my folks. My mother made one of those big pots of spaghetti sauce that simmers all afternoon. The kind Frank liked so much. She doesn't usually take the time these days. It tasted the way I remembered.

Supper on the plane back to Montreal was Rotini alla Bolognese. In a plastic dish covered with tinfoil. Bleached and stained with industrial red sauce, dotted with nuggets of something that might have been meat once but wasn't anymore.

I didn't bother eating.

Piano Lesson

I finally saw *The Piano*, that richly gothic story of a woman sent from Scotland to marry a settler in New Zealand.

The heroine, played by Holly Hunter, hasn't spoken since she was a child. She brings her surrogate voice, a piano, to the wilderness with her. But when she arrives, her new husband won't haul it off the beach and drag it to their little house in the Antipodes.

Big mistake.

Another settler, played by Harvey Keitel, whose nose is niftily decorated with Maori tattoos, rescues the instrument and carries it to his cabin. He hires her to teach him how to play, then offers to return the piano in exchange for sex. New Zealand's first lay-away plan. My way or the Steinway.

I have a quibble which has nothing to do with piano lessons—there's nothing to eat in this movie. Nobody leers over a haunch of New Zealand spring lamb, nobody drools over a plate of wichitty grubs. The fact is, nobody gets any grub all movie long.

Okay, Holly Hunter's daughter eats a piece of dry toast, but toast isn't really food. And yes, there is a row of wishbones strung over the hearth in Harvey Keitel's cabin, but you never actually see him dining. It's as if he'd kept score for a while and then got bored. Keitel 7, Chickens 0.

Maybe these people were fasting.

Maybe they had the same flu which flattened my usual good spirits a few days ago, taking with it my energy and my appetite. Lately, I'm down to a slice of toast, a little clear broth, and a handful of aspirins a day. This is unlike me.

I've never fasted willingly. Once when I was a kid I went three days without eating, but that was because I was on the road and my money ran out in Hamilton, and I was too proud to beg.

On the first day, I imagined meals to eat. On the second, I tried to take a bite out of a chestnut that had fallen from a tree. On the third, I stole a tomato from somebody's garden, an act which left me so completely exhausted, I spent the rest of the day sleeping.

Someone finally wired me a bit of cash. I hauled my starved self to a restaurant, ordered two big breakfasts and couldn't finish one of them.

This was a big disappointment.

Three days without food is no big deal on the world hunger scale, but ever since Hamilton, I've been more sympathetic toward those who don't have enough to eat. I'm also more inclined to appreciate those who have the courage to fast for political purposes.

I worked up north for some years as a manager of journalists. One day, we heard that a woman in one of the small communities had gone on a hunger strike in protest against the federal government. It sounded serious. We called her on the phone.

The woman said she was angry because Brian Mulroney was spying on her through the television set. Welcome to the weird zone.

She told us she wasn't going to eat again. Not until she got tired of caribou tea and bannock. Wait a minute, we said, that's no hunger strike. She said yes, it certainly was—caribou tea and bannock don't count as real food.

End of story.

Sometimes a fast is in the belly of the beholder, and sometimes you simply get the flu. I was hoping mine would be over with quickly. Fat chance. Appetite is crawling back to me with all the speed of a piano being dragged through the jungle.

After the movie, we went home and ate chicken baked with garlic. It was all I could do to pick at mine; unlike Harvey Keitel, I didn't save the wishbone.

MEAT MEETS MYTH IN THE MOVIES

Hercules is hanging out in the countryside uprooting trees and throwing giant boulders in the air. He's clearing the land and working on his lats and delts. It's hot. He's oiled, he's pumped.

The sea is so blue he squints. He's a hero at home on the Aegean. A giant pig roasts on a spit nearby. Smoke from the fire rises straight to the fragrant heavens. Surely, he thinks, this pleases the gods.

Suddenly there's a noise, a whimper, a bleating lamb perhaps. He sees nothing among the boulders, nothing in the low bushes.

But wait. There's that sound again. Could it be…a woman?

He strains his eyes in the ocean's glare. There she is, helpless, exhausted from a shipwreck. More than woman, surely this is a goddess. She's beautiful. Her flimsy dress is torn. Her shoulders are white as spilled milk. She's barely conscious.

Hercules picks her up. She faints in his arms as he carries her off. What fate awaits? Remember, this is hundreds of years before date rape, and he's got that look in his eye.

But no. He carries her to the fire and lays her down beside one of the giant, uprooted trees. He sits alone on the other side of the fire, tending his roasting pig and staring into the distance. What a gent!

Hours pass. She opens one eye. Where is she? Who is this muscle-bound oaf? She mustn't let him know she's awake. She must escape!

She runs off while he's poking the fire. He grunts. Women!

She doesn't get far. There's nowhere to go. And slowly, she is lured back to the fire by the smell of that pig. (No, not Hercules; the pig on the grill, silly!) She comes back. He knew she would.

It's obvious she hasn't eaten for days. No words are spoken. He offers his wineskin. She wrinkles her nose at the thought of drinking from a disgusting leather bag of god knows what. Still, she swallows greedily. The wine runs down her chin and over her breasts.

Hercules is too much a man not to notice, and much too cool to be obvious about it. But it's easy to see what he thinks. Her navel would make a fine goblet. It's enough to make a strong man weep.

She hands him back the wineskin. Whatever it was, at least it was wet. But it's not enough; she's starving, and she smells barbecue.

Her nostrils twitch. Hercules bids her sit. The pig, basted with oil and brushed with rosemary, is sweet and tender. He brings her the entire thing, still on the spit, and motions for her to chow down. She grimaces. Hey, lady, there are no knives and forks here, this is the damn wilderness!

White Shoulders takes the tiniest mouthful and chews greedily, daintily. Herc's arms strain. He holds the pig until she eats her fill.

Then—get this—he goes back to his side of the fire with the pig still in his arms. He strikes an oiled pose, leers at her with sophistication and says "I will eat where your lips have touched!"

She rolls her eyes.

This is my all-time favourite food scene from the movies.

Hercules. Italy, 1959. Directed by Lewis Coates (Luigi Cozzi, actually.) Steve Reeves starred in the title role, with Sylva Koscina as the woman. Available on video, it's so bad it's good. But you don't need to rent the movie to be like Hercules. All you need is a bottle of retsina, some barbecue, and a partner with white shoulders. You simply eat where your lover's lips have touched.

BITTER GREENS

You can leaf through a cookbook at the bookstore and take notes when the clerk's not looking. You can rip a page out of one of those better living magazines at your dentist's. As a last resort, you can call your mom long-distance. But if you really pay attention, you can pick up a recipe anywhere.

Last week I was in one of those big supermarkets. I needed to stock up on some of the basics. I also needed some water, which was advertised on sale at thirty cents a bottle cheaper than the dépanneur near my place.

Bottled water is a staple if you can't stand the taste or the smell of the stuff that flows out of your taps.

While I was shopping I took a turn down the produce aisle. They had a spectacular display of chicory. Big green bunches of the stuff, looking like dandelions on drugs. And I was suddenly struck with the urge for a little more bitterness in my life. There's never enough bitterness in my life. So I tossed a head in my cart and wheeled it over to the checkout counter.

The guy at the till was a pro. His name—Gino—was stitched to the breast of his jacket. He knew what he was doing. There'd be no thumping of fruit today. No putting the soap next to the butter. All the bar codes were going to beep on the first pass. Gino was smooth and efficient, from soup to nuts.

But when he came to the greens he paused. He was puzzled. His eyes narrowed. He knew what they were, but the name wouldn't come, and he didn't know what to punch in. His rhythm was off, and there was still a conveyor-belt of groceries to check.

Finally, he waved at the kid bagging tins at the next counter. "What's this?" he asked. The kid looked up and said "Chicory."

Gino punched it in with one of those "I-shoulda-known" looks on his face.

"Hey," I said, "you're an Italian guy. You should know chicory."

"Yeah," he agreed "We used to eat this stuff all the time when I was a kid."

"How?" I expected him to say in salads. He surprised me.

He said "My mother used to boil it. Then she'd dress it with a bit of olive oil and some lemon juice. It's great with a piece of steak."

He was right. This is what you do. Trim the leaves and blanch them in boiling water. Drain, and toss them with the oil and lemon in a three–to–one ratio. Nothing to it. Maybe add a bit of salt. The taste is sharp and adult, with just enough bitterness to keep your palate clean.

You needn't spend a lot of money for the steak. Ask your butcher for a bavette. It's an oddly shaped flap of meat from the loin, tougher than a T-bone or a faux-filet. But it's juicier and twice as tasty, and the reason you don't always see it is because the butcher often keeps it for himself. Sauté it over high heat in a cast iron frying pan with a bit of dried rosemary. No oil and just a little salt in the pan.

All you need to finish your plate is some red potatoes mashed with butter or chicken stock and a quarter-cup of asiago cheese. Or maybe some warm cannellini beans, puréed with olive oil and garlic.

Thanks for the recipe, Gino.

A Kick in the Ribs

The best story I know about barbecue has to do with Bobby Seale, the former Black Panther. You may remember him. He was arrested with a handful of Yippies and proto-revolutionaries for trying to disrupt the Democratic National Convention in Chicago in 1968.

Seale's the one who interrupted the judge, repeatedly and correctly, if somewhat rudely, at the start of the proceedings. So the judge ordered Seale bound to his chair and gagged for the duration of the trial.

Justice is blind, and prefers its defendants mute.

Well, time passes. Even revolutionaries have to make a living. Over the years, the Chicago Seven alumni have taken a variety of dizzy approaches to making a fast buck. Eldridge Cleaver once tried to market a line of trousers which featured a prominent codpiece. Jerry Rubin became a stockbroker.

Tom Hayden married an actress and went into California politics. So did Ronald Reagan, come to think of it, although Hayden's ex, Jane Fonda, was a marginally better actor than Nancy Davis. Then again, Reagan did better with the voters.

Fast forward to 1988. Seale writes a cookbook called *Barbeque'n With Bobby*. It's full of good advice. "Do not use gasoline or other volatile substances. They are dangerous and may explode." And "Do not spray lighter fluid on already hot coals."

He should know.

Like me, Seale uses a kettle barbecue. Unlike me, he uses hickory wood to flavour what he's cooking. I use apple wood. The last time I was out in the Eastern Townships I stopped at an orchard, bought some cider, and asked the orchard guy if he had any deadwood laying around. He was happy to be rid of it. He had that look on his face. I could tell what he was thinking. Boy, those city folk are getting stranger every year.

The joke's on him. Think global, and barbecue local. Apple smoke is sophisticated and subtle. If Mr. Farmer were so smart, he'd be chipping the wood and bagging it and selling it for a fancy price by the side of the road.

But let's get back to barbecue. Soak a piece of apple, or any other hardwood, in water. When the coals are ready, lay on the wood. It will smoulder slowly, because it's been soaked. Put your meat on the grill. Make sure the meat is not directly over the coals. You want the flavour of woodsmoke, not charred fat.

If you don't have access to hardwood, you can use onion peels. You can use a handful of chives. You can use your imagination.

If you have a gas barbecue with a lid, you can use the same technique. Keep the meat away from the flame. Add some soaked hardwood chips to give the meat a bit of smoke. Keep the lid closed.

If you have a hibachi, I can't help you.

The best advice in Bobby's book has to do with barbecue sauce.

You can baste your meat with a marinade when it's cooking, but do not under any circumstances paint your ribs or wings with a barbecue sauce that has sugar and tomato in it; not until the meat is nearly done. Sugar burns, and so does tomato.

It's not a pleasant taste.

Barbeque'n With Bobby earned Seale an appointment as a judge at a rib-cooking contest in Cleveland some years ago. Bobby, ever the entrepreneur, ordered vast quantities of ribs to barbecue and sell on his own. He wrote a cheque for the ribs in the amount of $7,767.13. It bounced.

A warrant was issued for his arrest.

Burn, baby, burn.

MOONSHINE, BRIGHTLY

There's a bottle of home-made grappa in my cupboard. It looks like tapwater, and it tastes like grape kerosene, but a weakness for home-made booze runs in the family. It's a tradition that goes back a long way.

My relatives were poor when they came to Canada a hundred years ago. To survive, they cut a bit of wood, they did a little hunting, they grew a little food. They lived on a farm in the bush. To make some extra cash, my uncle Tony made bootleg whiskey.

You might call him a moonshiner. I prefer to think of him as a boutique distiller. He grew his own high-quality ingredients. His still was custom-built according to traditional specifications. He even made his own deliveries, just like the Bronfmans. But unlike Mr. Sam, my Uncle Tony wasn't in it to get rich. He was simply trying to earn a bit of off-farm income.

Tony ran his booze to the hotels in town once a week down a network of narrow back roads. He used his cousin's Chalmers touring car, a huge roadster whose front seat had been hollowed out and custom-fitted with a secret tank.

During the height of the summer season sometime in the early Twenties, Tony heard that the cops were onto him. He had a run to make, so he asked my father to come for a ride. My father was five years old at the time.

A ride in the car was a treat, but Tony made it paradise—he gave my little dad a whole pack of gum to chew. Tony said "Put all of this gum in your mouth. If anybody makes me stop the car, you stop chewing. And if anybody asks you anything, you just nod yes or no. Got that?" My five-year old dad stuffed his cheek and nodded happily, and off they drove.

Sure enough, the provincial police were waiting for them on a little cowpath of a road. The cops smiled and put their hands on their guns. They said "We got you now, Tony. The jig is up. We want to search the car."

"Hey, you got it wrong," said Tony. "I'm taking my little brother to the dentist. He's got a bad tooth. Take a look at him."

The cops peered closely at my little dad, who was sitting scared in the front seat of the car. One of the cops said "Jesus, will you take a look at this."

My little dad's jaw looked swollen. "Does it hurt, sonny?" My dad nodded. "Are you going to the dentist, sonny?" My dad nodded. "Is he going to pull your tooth?" My dad nodded again.

"That's a brave little kid," said the cops, smiling kindly. "Tony, you better get him to town right away."

Tony took off, laughing to himself as moonshine sloshed in the hidden tank.

That was my old man's introduction to rum-running. He's over seventy now, and while it's fair to say that booze did him more harm than good over the years—in the final analysis, all my relatives are better consumers than producers—the old man did teach me how to drink.

We could have a glass of anything when we were kids. It was never a big deal. There was no moralizing. We learned to drink it, just as we learned to make it.

I discovered moderation at home where it was safe. The taste of liquor didn't trip me up when I got old enough to do my first stupid things.

Oddly, in recent years my old man's grown allergic to drink. It makes him sneeze, and he swells up. This may be a cosmic balancing of the books, but I think it's sad. It means the loss of one more pleasure, at an age when he needs all the pleasure he can get.

And it's sad for another reason. I've got my eye on some copper coils. If I decide to make a little moonshine of my own, I want an experienced palate to judge the final product. And maybe to help me rig my Honda with a secret tank.

THE LAST SUPPER

The condemned man ate a hearty meal. Never mind what he ate for a moment; consider simply that he was about to die in jail, and that he had an appetite.

Death is supposed to focus the mind, but I like to think mine would focus more on "How the hell can I get out of here?" and less on "What's for lunch?"

I read an article once, about last meals ordered by men on Death Row. Pizza featured large, as did red Jello and quarts of cola, entire apple pies, buckets of fried chicken with secret herbs and spices, and cartons of chocolate milk. Yum.

I used to think a menu like that was proof enough of guilt.

Given the choice, god forbid, most of us like to think we'd opt for something more elaborate, an elegant meal with lots of courses served on white linen with real silver.

Don't be so easily duped. Logistics aren't in your favour. Soufflé isn't easily delivered to a prison. And a fancy dish gone wrong would be the final disappointment. What are you going to do, send it back? I'd crack. Take me now, and never mind the hood, let's get this over with.

I say a slice of pizza looks like a good bet if you're sitting in jail—delivery's guaranteed, and you know it's going to taste the same from one end of the country to the other.

But most of us want more of a gastronomic choice than "Hold the anchovies." After all, there's plenty of stuff to eat that even a prison couldn't screw up. Bring me a bottle of red wine, a half-pound slice of blue cheese, a loaf of bread and some sweet butter.

The last time I ate like that was in May of 1974. I remember it perfectly well. It was a payday. I stopped on the way home from work and bought a nice chianti. Then I went to a nearby cheese store for a slice of gorgonzola, and finally to the bakery for a loaf of fresh bread.

Paradise doesn't come any cheaper.

Two hours later I was on the floor, on my hands and knees, trying to keep still while something tightened a vice around my temples and something else pushed a long, hot needle into my left eye. The evening light falling through the window was so bright I couldn't look at it, and the sound of my breathing was so loud it hurt my ears.

When the telephone rang, I fell forward in agony and crawled towards it on my hands and knees. I don't remember who it was. I remember asking the caller to phone my family doctor. I remember weeping.

My first migraine.

I have pills now to control the pain. But I gave up blue cheese for good, and it's only recently that I've dared to take the occasional sip of red wine.

Twenty years later, I still haven't got the nerve to try the two together.

But if I were about to die? Bring me blue cheese from every nation that makes it, creamy and soft and marbled deeply with iridescent veins. Bring me a bottle of dark red wine, tannic and heavy and purple in the glass. And a pound of sweet butter, and a loaf of the best bread from the bakery nearest Death Row.

Let me eat in peace, ya lousy coppers! Quit that praying, padre, you're making too much noise! Warden, all I ask is that when the pain begins, you throw the switch.

Oatmeal Cookie Theology

One morning in the first grade, when I still believed there was a God and I was sure I had a soul, I screwed up all my courage and asked Sister St. Martin two simple questions. "Where's my soul? And Sister, what does it look like?"

It was the question she'd been waiting for all her life. She whirled to face me, pointed to her heart and said "It's here!" Then she whirled around again, and in a fit of Zen Catholicism, she slapped a dirty eraser against the blackboard. When the chalk dust cleared, I saw a shadowy, oblong mark.

"It looks like that!" she said. The mark she made looked like a piece of shredded wheat. It was one of those moments of revelation, as when the monk asked the master "What is greater than the Buddha?" and the master answers "Buns!"

It made no sense. It was satori in reverse. I didn't feel enlightenment, I felt a vague and sinking darkness. From that moment I held the firm belief that there was a piece of breakfast cereal deep inside my chest, and if I wasn't careful, some morning in the future my shredded wheat soul was going to be scraped from the bowl of my self and thrown away.

Ever since then, I've never been able to look at a bowl of cereal—no shredded wheat, no Froot Loops or Count Chocula, not even the rice that's shot from guns—without remembering the shock of chalk dust on the blackboard. In fact, the only cereal I really enjoy without an onrush of religious melancholy is oatmeal. But not just plain old oatmeal. I mean the oatmeal in a cookie.

For a taste of Zen, cream one cup plus two tablespoons of butter in a mixing bowl. In a separate bowl, stir and toss together two and a half cups of rolled oats, half a cup of wheat germ, a cup of flour, a pinch of salt, and a cup plus two tablespoons of dark brown sugar.

Add the dry ingredients to the bowl with the butter. Dissolve a teaspoon of baking soda in a quarter-cup of boiling water and throw that in. Add a teaspoon of vanilla and mix everything together very well.

It will make a loose dough. Don't worry about that. Place generous teaspoonfuls a couple of inches apart on greased cookie sheets. Flatten slightly with your fingertips and bake in a preheated 375°F oven for ten minutes or so. The cookies will spread, and their edges will turn a light caramel colour. Take them from the oven, remove them from the sheets with a spatula and let them cool on racks.

Make a pot of tea and consider this. A Buddhist monk once asked a master for instruction. The master asked if the monk had eaten his rice. The monk replied that he had. The master said "Then wash your bowl!"

Bingo.

A Word About Oranges

In the 14th century, the men who dived for gems in the lakes of Ceylon rubbed their bodies with the oil from orange peels. They believed the smell of the oil would repel crocodiles. If those crocodiles could have prayed, I imagine they would have given thanks for a food so wondrous it seasoned itself.

John McPhee, the best feature reporter in the English-speaking world, has written a lovely little book called, simply, *Oranges*. He says the sweetest orange is one grown nearest the equator. An orange grown high on the tree is sweeter than one grown close to the ground, and an orange on the furthest reaches of a limb is sweeter than one grown further in. The blossom end of any orange is sweeter than the stem end. I dream of that half of that orange.

The word itself comes to us from the Hindu *naranga*, meaning "perfume within." It went to the Persians as *narandj* and to the Byzantines as *nerantzion*. In Latin it became *aurantia*. The Spanish say *naranja*, and the Italians *arancia*. The smallest orange is the kumquat. *Kam kwat* means "golden orange" in Cantonese.

The citizens of Nome, Alaska, drink 12,000 quarts of Florida orange juice each month. Los Angelenos drink a quarter-million quarts of juice from Florida, which surely counts as one of the greatest triumphs of marketing over common sense.

A warm orange yields the most juice. You could, if you wished, pour boiling water over unpeeled oranges and let them sit five minutes before juicing them.

The rinds from industrial juice oranges are processed into cattle fodder. The peels are chopped, then tumbled in dryers. Imagine those cows, breathing deeply. What ice cream could be made from their milk!

Archers used to make their bows from orange wood. Someone should have told William Tell. He might have chosen another fruit to place on his son's head.

The French poet Jacques Prévert wrote of "an orange on the table, your dress on the floor and you in my bed." Prévert was no fool.

I dislike regret, but I'm not happy about the year-round availability of tangerines. I'd prefer it if we could do without them until Christmas, and do without them again after February. In spite of this wish, I can't resist a tangerine and I'll buy one whenever I see one. I gain the fulfilment of my craving, but I've lost that child-like sense of anticipation.

My son holds the record in our family for the consumption of tangerines. We were living in the Arctic, and we came south for Christmas with my folks. We hadn't seen any decent fresh fruit in months. He sat down by a bowl of tangerines and disposed of nine of them, one after the other, with a hunger that made me wonder if I'd done right to take him north in the first place.

If you want, you can make a good enough salad from two oranges in a vinaigrette with lettuce, half a sliced red onion, some oregano and a handful of black, oil-cured olives.

You can put orange peel into beef stew along with your bouquet garni. You can squeeze a little juice in your fresh tomato soup; add a little orange zest while you're at it. Or try this, as recommended by Lorenza de' Medici in her book, *The Renaissance of Italian Cooking*—peel two oranges, finely slice the peel, blanch it in boiling water for two minutes, and drain. Sauté a finely chopped onion in four tablespoons of olive oil. Add the drained peel to the oil, along with a cup-and-a-half of pitted black olives. Remove from the heat. Cook a pound of spaghetti in a pot of salted boiling water until it's *al dente*. Dress the spaghetti with the olive mixture, add four more tablespoons of oil, and be grateful the Moors invaded Italy.

If you want to make a humble little lamp, carefully slice and peel an orange around its equator. You will have two equal shells; place a candle in the lower half, cut a small hole in the top half of the orange peel, to allow the flame to breathe. Light the candle and put the top lid on. Your lamp will cast a faint and pleasing glow, and it will perfume your room.

Here is a way of eating oranges for dessert: peel and slice four of them, dress them with three or four tablespoons of sugar, the zest of a lemon, the juice of two oranges, and the juice of the lemon. Let them sit at least four hours, and serve with almond cookies.

Your friends will think you're a genius. They could be right.

If You Knew Sushi

I took a friend for sushi once, an act that was both an essay in cross-cultural bridging and the gustatory equivalent of a pun. My friend is an Inuk from the Northwest Territories. The Inuit like their fish raw.

We were looking for some supper after a boring, day-long meeting. We wanted something good to eat. After all, when you work in the north and you have a chance to come south, you want to dine especially well. Good restaurants are hard to come by in the Arctic.

What to eat was an issue. Mike wasn't sure he wanted curry, and I knew he wasn't nuts about spaghetti. We didn't feel like steaks. Sushi with an Inuk seemed right to me, even if it was a bit like coals to Newcastle for Mike. Or rather, raw fish to Rankin Inlet.

We went to a place that had been highly recommended. It was packed, but there were two spots at the sushi bar. We sat down.

As you know, the Inuit and the Japanese share certain physical characteristics. The similarities may be rooted in pre-history. The native people of Japan are the Ainu. The Ainu word for fire is similar to the Inuktitut word for wood, and the Ainu word for horse is similar to the Inuktitut word for travel. Be that as it may, my friend Mike was pegged as Japanese as soon as we walked in.

We were treated with deference by the top knife, a handsome fellow dressed in costume and wearing one of those samurai bandanas. He gave Mike the sort of nod one insider gives another, and then he got down to business.

He sliced a piece of tuna into edible haiku, working with the precise economy of gesture shared by all artists, whether they are stretching a canvas, tuning a carburetor or slicing fish.

We ate well and I could tell that, although the raw food wasn't a novelty, Mike was impressed with the neatness of the little bundles put before us. Even if the wasabi made him sneeze.

The sushi man decided that my friend was a connoisseur, however; every time he put a bit of food before us, he'd look at Mike and speak a word or two of Japanese. Presumably he was asking about the food. How the hell did I know. How the hell did Mike.

But Mike had the presence of mind to nod in appreciation and to bark out "hai!" whenever he thought it was appropriate. This seemed to satisfy the sushi man.

When we'd eaten our fill and finished our beer, we declined tea and I asked for the bill. As we got up to leave, the sushi man directed a stream of rapid-fire Japanese at us. He was very animated. He nodded to the counter where he'd been slicing tuna, he made hummingbird gestures with his hands. He clearly wanted Mike's opinion.

Mike did the only thing he could. He bowed to the man and said, slowly and carefully, as if English was his second language (which, in fact, it is) "Thank you so very much."

Mike and I went for a walk, and we talked about culture and skewed perceptions and the curious things that people eat. For example, many Inuit can't stand the thought of cheese, although they'll eat the half-digested contents of the stomach of a freshly slaughtered walrus. Go figure.

We ended up at a movie, one of those silly adventure pictures. The hero dines with a group of bad guys who are eating monkey brains from skulls, and soup with eyeballs floating in it. I said the thought of it repelled me. Mike said "Me, too."

Then he checked himself. He looked at me and laughed.

"Wait a minute," he said. "We eat stuff like that."

WORST MEALS

This is an embarrassing admission, but certain foods trip my gag reflex. Fava beans. Vanilla pudding. Liver does it almost every time, as does lamb, a distressing variety of seafoods, and anything buried in a cheese sauce. You get the picture.

My list is arbitrary and idiosyncratic. I'll bet yours is, too. Unless you're an omnivore. Even if you are, there are probably things you won't eat willingly.

The worst meal I've ever eaten started with snails in a cream sauce, proceeded to raw scallops and a salad which emphasized several kinds of highly assertive fungus. We finished with an especially gooey, creamy-rich trifle.

What are you going to do if your host can't compose a menu? I took small bites. I ate a lot of bread. I took many little sips of wine, and left small bits of things uneaten on my plate. I smiled and tried to look interested in the conversation. All through supper I picked and dawdled and considered my failings as a human being and a guest. Why hadn't I learned to like this kind of stuff when I was a kid? I went for a burger when the coast was clear, to cleanse my palate.

It was a miserable experience, and it took me back to childhood, when I had to sit at the kitchen table and eat until my plate was clean. I used to bring my rosary case to the supper table with me, just to be on the safe side. We might have been having fish boiled in milk.

If so, when no one was looking, I'd pack my rosary case with all the disgusting bits, and then I'd head out to play. I dumped the evidence in a different spot every time, to lessen the likelihood of getting caught.

I think we react this way to food when we're young because our palates are so pure. Our mouths are sensitive, our tastebuds have yet to be wrecked by booze or cigarettes. If we get lucky, age dulls us to the point where we can enjoy whatever's put in front of us. But sometimes it doesn't, and our childhood food traumas stay with us, unreasonably, forever.

For example, I don't care how much tomato sauce you put on polenta, I still won't eat it willingly. Polenta is an Italian corn-meal mush, one of the comfort foods of the ancients. You can buy ready-made tubes of it in Italian grocery stores. Lots of people love it. Not me. I ate too much of it when I was young. I left home so I wouldn't have to eat it any more.

Nor will I eat any of those frozen dinners. My parents held down two jobs apiece while I was growing up—we were not the typical Fifties family. Mom had four boys, and she tried to give herself a break whenever she could. So when Swanson came out with the frozen TV Dinner, she thought she'd try one out on me. I remember it well. Turkey with mashed potatoes and yellow gravy and corn niblets, and a variety of unidentifiable chemical tastes. I ate it all, and then I got sick. No more TV Dinners at our house.

I admit to a lot of idiosyncrasies when it comes to what's on my plate. Sometimes this is a problem. The woman I dine with requires lamb from time to time. To her, it's the taste of home. Unfortunately whenever I try lamb, I taste the mutton it was meant to be. Lamb in the house overpowers me, there's nothing I can do. Bless her heart, she orders it rare when we eat out.

She'll also eat a steak tartare from time to time. Not me, even though I spent several years working in the Arctic, where raw meat is a way of life. I tried raw seal once. Also raw caribou and raw char. Once each. Those were swallows which took courage. You know how it is when you're a guest. You swallow hard and try to be polite.

I was always embarrassed by this. But one day I overheard a group of Inuit women. They were storytellers, chatting merrily in the green room at the radio station where I worked. They were eating chunks of frozen caribou, drinking tea and laughing before they went on air. I asked one of them what was so funny.

She said, between giggles, that she couldn't help it, but whenever she took a bite of white people's food, she felt like she was going to heave it right back up.

I told her I knew what she meant.

CONFESSIONS OF A BAG-BOY

Red slices of field tomato on a bed of cold, sweet lettuce leaves, crossed with strips of smoky bacon, sandwiched between two thick slices of sour rye, the whole thing painted with mayonnaise— I used to be a sucker for a BLT.

Then I got a summer job in a supermarket.

After swabbing floors and stocking shelves, bagging groceries, cleaning up after the meat guys in their stupid hats, and turning the peaches bruise-side down, it was my job to rescue the lettuce.

Big soggy boxes full of big rotten heads came in by the filthy truckload from the fields of California. We unloaded the boxes roughly, tossing them across the shaft of sunlight that fell between the back of the truck and the wet, black floor of the loading dock.

Lettuce stinks. The boxes were greasy with rot, and we handled them with gloves. I never used those gloves for anything but lettuce. We smoked when we worked. The smoke killed the smell.

Some of the boxes we threw in dank corners. Others we tore open, to begin the mucky business of cleaning the heads for display. There was a lot of remedial tearing of wilt, until we found leaves that looked passably crisp. We sliced the stems with a knife, so they'd look milky-white. We stood ankle-deep in lettuce slime.

I gave up BLT's immediately. In fact, the only vegetables I ate while I was working there were ones I could peel or pour out of a can. I used to look at people eating lettuce and think "If you only knew…"

The word lettuce comes from the Latin *lac* for milk, and *lactuca*, a Latin form of the leaf, so-called because of the milky stuff that dripped from its roots when cut. This was the lettuce used for Caesar's salad. Who gave a damn? I just wanted to rip leaves, slice

100

bottoms, and wash the heads with a hose as fast as I could, to get rid of the stink.

We dealt with rotten produce in the morning, before the shoppers arrived. In the afternoon I loaded cars with groceries. We had a simple system. The customer would pull up in a car and hand you a fistful of ticket stubs. You looked for the duplicates among the tubs of groceries on the conveyor belt, and gave the person those groceries. It was foolproof.

One afternoon I was loading a woman's car. It was so hot that, for the first time, I envied the blood-covered butchers hacking merrily at their meat. At least they were cool. I was tired. I was trying to work fast, so I could get back to the air conditioning.

The woman had a big order. I broke my back filling her trunk with bags of groceries, and piling them on her back seat.

I was nearly done when three more tubs came hurtling down the line. I looked up and asked her "Those yours, too, ma'am?" She smiled sweetly, quickly. "Yes, they are."

I put them on the front seat. I put them on the floor between the front seat and the back. I put them wherever I could. She gave me a tip, and pulled away, smiling. She had barely enough room to shift gears. Nice lady. I waved goodbye.

As she drove off, another car pulled up. A guy in a hurry gave me his stubs. I said "Hi, your groceries aren't out yet. I'll just go inside to see what the holdup is." There were no more groceries waiting. And I remembered the woman's smile.

Uh-oh.

I went to find the boss.

He looked at me hard. He apologized to the man, and let him do his shopping again for nothing. He took the man's word for everything he said he'd bought.

Nice guy, my boss. He could have fired me. Instead, he looked at me without expression for the next two weeks. Until I quit and went back to school.

I threw my stinking lettuce gloves in the trash on the way out. But it was six months before I could even think of putting some L in a BLT.

I've washed my lettuce carefully ever since. And I always count the bags of groceries when the bag-boy loads my car.

Dinners With Daddies

The first of the men whose daughters I dated made paper at the mill. Etienne was tall and skinny, and his smile was sharp and quick and genuine. He was handsome the way men are handsome in old movies. He had short black hair and a pencil-thin moustache.

He also had a sense of humour, rare among the fathers of my dates. Maybe that was my fault. Maybe if I had daughters I wouldn't have much to laugh about, either. Nevertheless.

He was a little deaf; paper machines make a lot of noise, and he glared when you spoke softly, which I tend to do. But I always thought he heard what he wanted to hear, when it suited him to hear it.

He had the habit of chewing gum. Once when I was invited there for supper, he was the first to come to the table. He took his place and put his napkin on before anyone else could sit down. And quick as that, he took a piece of gum from his mouth and stuck it behind his ear and reached to pour a glass of milk.

The gesture was automatic—gum out, rolled once, tucked away. All in one movement, as if he'd done it a thousand times. I gaped for a millisecond and then sat down, but everyone saw that I'd seen what he'd done.

His wife stiffened in a little fit of disapproval. The girl I was dating blushed, her little sisters giggled. I'd been nervous, but the gum behind the ear was a sweet, unconscious gesture. I felt as if I'd been given a gift. As if he'd done what he did to put me at ease.

On the other hand, whenever I came to pick her up, if he was sleeping in his chair, I always snuck a look. He nearly always had a piece of gum behind his lobe.

His daughter and I were serious; the first one always is. But after we'd dated a couple of years, Etienne's wife decided that I didn't have a future with her daughter. It seems to me she made her daughter ditch me, and that was the end of the roast beef dinners.

The next one was Norwegian.

Carl sold Scandinavian trinkets, high-end stuff and tchotchkes from a little store that was painted with blue flowers. He was taciturn and prone to moods, but it was hard to tell what mood he was really in because his chief expression, at least when I was in his company, was an absence of expression. When he smiled you'd think the sun was shining, but he rarely smiled at me.

He had a housekeeper for a time, after his wife took off and left him with the kids. The housekeeper was a short, square woman he'd brought over from the old country. There were rumours about the nature of Carl's relationship with her, and why she didn't work for him any more, and why she wouldn't speak to him if she saw him in the street. The rumours suggested she misunderstood the nature of the arrangement.

Carl seemed to me to be suspicious of food, although he always ate the treats Norwegians eat—lutefisk, with gusto; lingonberries and pancakes; and gjetöst by the block. I'd try a piece whenever he hauled it out, but I never really liked it. It's the only cheese I've ever tried that tastes of wax and peanuts. He kept an apartment above the store. It smelled like perfumed candles, and I don't remember ever having supper with him there.

Carl's daughter and I married quickly, and he gave us a wedding present from the store, something he had on the shelf. It doesn't matter what it was. His daughter turned out to be as flighty as he was glum, but I was very much in love with her and we had a son in the brief time we were together. It went by in a blur, and I've forgotten most of the worst of it.

The last of the fathers of daughters invented Everlasting Tuna.

Donald was a research chemist. He helped develop Pampers in the Fifties. He was one of those tall, skinny men who tinker, and he had a lot of theories about the way things worked. His theories were different from mine.

He sailed whenever he could to places where it was warm. His boat was small, and once or twice I was invited to go with them, but I never went.

On one of these trips he caught a tuna and cooked it in a pot. There was no way to keep anything cold on the boat, so he ate and reheated, and ate and reheated, the fish. For days. Without refrigeration. On the theory that boiling overcomes spoiling.

A helluva theory.

He and I never really got along. His daughter knew that and so did I, but if Donald did, he was decent enough to keep it to himself because I made his daughter happy. He died of cancer last year, and I made quarts and quarts of chicken broth for him during the long months when soup was the only thing he could keep down.

There are no daddies after him.

THE REAL CIPAILLE

We'd just come from language school in Jonquière, and we were taking a glum vacation on the Gaspé coast. We were looking at the cliffs, and trying our new French on strangers. We weren't talking to each other very much because it seemed as if we argued constantly.

I was also looking for a restaurant which served the real cipaille, with partridge and wild game. But every time we stopped and asked for some, we were told there was none this week. There'd been some the week before and there might be some next week, but nobody had any now. We didn't have the time to wait.

It was a difficult vacation. There were many things unsettled in our lives then, and somewhere between Barachois and Percé, all our honest differences of opinion began to look like betrayals.

We weren't talking when I killed the dog. It was a black pup. It ran onto the highway, wagging its tail. I didn't swerve. Not at that speed. We felt a heavy thump. I stopped the car.

The pup lay on the pavement and tried to crawl. Its back was broken. When Susan picked it up, the puppy licked her hand. She was crying. I tried to speak. There was nothing I could say.

A man came out from behind his garage. His face was set hard.

Is there a vet nearby, we asked. We'll pay whatever it costs.

I'll take care of this, he said.

Susan gave him the puppy. By now it was trembling. Where is the vet, she asked again, we'll take him to the vet.

I'll take care of this, said the man. He smiled without smiling. It was clear what he meant. There were plenty of other black puppies running loose in his yard.

There was nothing we could do. Susan was crying, and I asked myself a hundred times if there wasn't some way I could have swerved. It's a question I still ask.

We spent that night in a motel in Percé. There were many things unsettled between us, and now there was this business of the dog.

The next morning I went out in the fog and took photos of the Percé rock while Susan was having coffee. For a moment I wondered whether I should just drive on alone. After all, I was too quick to find fault. I was unwilling to give an inch. And now I'd killed a dog. Maybe I should just drive on.

I held the thought for a moment.

Then I took a deep breath, and went back to the motel. Eventually we took the ferry to P.E.I. and had a fine, off-season holiday. The tourists had gone away. Anne of Green Gables had been put to bed for the winter. We had the beaches to ourselves and the sadness began to fade.

We ate fresh fish every day. We thought about driving back along the Gaspé coast, for one more look at the cliffs and one more attempt to find cipaille. We didn't. I couldn't stop thinking about the dog.

I have a recipe for the real cipaille at home somewhere. I got it in Jonquière, but I haven't seen it for a while. I haven't really looked very hard. It's complicated and worth making, if you have a couple of partridge and some deer meat and a rabbit. If you're willing to take the leap of faith required to bake something overnight. If you're willing to eat that much meat buried in that many layers of pastry.

If you want, there's a scaled-down version with readily-available ingredients in Julian Armstrong's excellent cookbook, *A Taste of Quebec*. I'd try her recipe myself, if the black dog didn't haunt me.

Poker Night

Once a month, more or less, I play poker with a group that includes two novelists, a short story writer, an editor, and one other poet besides me.

On the basis of winnings to date, short story writers play better poker than novelists, novelists play roughly as well as poets, and editors play better than anyone else. That last bit is not strictly true, but as someone who writes the occasional freelance piece, I feel it's important to suck up to editors.

We play basic poker. Stud, because it is a masculine game. And seven card high-low, which rewards the utterly bad hand. There are no wild cards in our games, and the stakes are so tiny that even the poets can afford to play. Nobody gets hurt. At least, no one gets hurt in the wallet.

Poker night is a chance for us to get together and talk to each other as men in the absence of women. It is Iron John without the bullshit.

We are not the Thanatopsis Inside Straight Poker Club, that card-playing subset of the Algonquin Round Table which included Heywood Broun, Robert Benchley and George S. Kaufman. In Howard Teichmann's biography, Kaufman is said to have quit a game in which his luck had run rotten all night by turning over his hand, which consisted mainly of twos and threes. Kaufman stood up and left the table, saying "I've been treydeuced."

We are not at that level of badinage, and twos and threes are often good enough to win in our game. But we value crisp wordplay and we aim equally high. You would expect as much from guys who make a living by turning important-sounding sentences into trifling sums of money.

An etiquette is evolving. Nobody smokes cigarettes; sometimes we smoke cigars, but we are a bunch of literary Clintons—we don't inhale. There's no hard liquor on the table. Everyone brings beer—one of the novelists makes his own, and usually brings enough for a round. The host is required to provide a fresh deck of cards, and enough junk food to last the evening.

Over the past few months, I've seen various bags of plain-flavoured chips, but no pickle-flavoured ones and no ketchup-flavoured ones. I've also seen pretzels, nuts and nachos. And plenty of those cheese things that look like orange packing foam.

Once I made a pot of chili adequate enough that the vegetarian among us ate two bowls. But real food is the exception, rather than the rule. There are no pickled eggs, no pickled onions and no pigs' knuckles. I have no idea what this means, unless it is that junk food is easier to swallow when all you have is a pair of threes.

Some years ago I played with a group of guys in my home town. We played the same games, but for smaller stakes—pennies then, as opposed to dimes now—but I'd have to say today's dime is yesterday's penny if you factor for inflation.

We had the same approach to food, with one variation. Someone always brought peppers. The hotter the better. We'd eat them and pretend our mouths weren't burning. "These are not so bad," we'd say. Tears would well up in our eyes. "I could take them even hotter than this," we'd say. Men in groups tell lies.

GQ Magazine once paid Martin Amis and four other writers £500 apiece to play poker for an evening. Each player then had to write an article about his experience for the magazine. Amis walked away from the table with £200 in winnings, which made his fee 25p a word. I'm getting about 12¢ a word for this.

Hey, it's more than I make writing poems.

A Gut Issue

As bellies go, it isn't one of the biggest. It is, however, a fine specimen. Rounded, almost apple-shaped. Protuberant, hard-looking and nuttily tanned.

The man who owns it sits on the steps of the library every morning and waits for the doors to open. He wears a sportcoat, even when it's hot. But his shirt is always open, and his fine brown belly is always ready to take advantage of the sun.

He has a snowy tonsure, a fringe of beard and an arrogant look. Some days I think he's an old writer, working on a final book. Or a péquiste researcher buttressing a private theory about those awful beans, gourgannes, which are the true test of the Québécois palate.

Maybe he's just one of those old men who have nothing better to do than leave their homes in the morning and go to read the obits in the library newspapers. And tan their very living bellies on the steps.

Once upon a time, a man called a belly like this his "front porch." Or his "corporation." He could pat it fondly, as if it were something other than himself, say a horse's flank, or his wife's behind. He'd strain against the buttons of his vest and say "It's bought and paid for!" Latterly, in this age of fitness, he calls it "Molson Muscle."

A man gets his belly from beer, from animal fat and easy living. He wears it proudly. What else is he going to do? In life, you learn to celebrate whatever you can't hide.

I used to work with a man whose belly was so big it sat on his lap when he sat down. He was a bulldozer operator. He looked like a jello statue with a hard hat and a cigar. His name was Peter.

After work, we drank in a bar in town. He drank free all night. Anyone who wanted to could balance a glass of draft on Peter's "porch." Peter would bend forward and pick up the glass in his teeth. He'd throw his head back and drain the glass dry without ever using his hands. Without ever spilling a drop.

He could do this two dozen times a night. If you wanted to see it, you could do so for the price of a glass of beer. Stupid people wanted to see it twice. They'd point at him and dig each other in the ribs and laugh as loud the second time. They'd clap him on the back. Peter didn't mind, as long as he wasn't buying.

Next day he'd jiggle horribly on the dozer, moving dirt, working the levers, leaning from side to side in his chair. The sweat ran off him in rivers. Heat was good, he said. It got him in shape for the bar.

I suppose these bellies are ugly. But the truth is—it's a cruel world—even the fattest man can camouflage his bulk in a well-cut three-piece suit. Unfortunately, women have nothing like this in which to hide their flesh.

But a man's belly, while it may be shaped like an apple, will kill him. It's too often sculpted from pastry cream desserts, and eggs in bacon grease. And beer.

A belly made of these is the outward sign of a heart about to break. Unless cancer gets there first, and whittles a man to a stick, whereupon the shrinking of his belly is profoundly sad, and spoken of in whispers.

WEDDING BELL BLUES

The bride, her sister and I were walking in the park. It was the day after the wedding, and the bride was kicking leaves. Her house had been overtaken by big women with square shoulders who'd come bearing pots of food left over from the wedding feast the night before.

The bride was dazed. Her sister and I had taken her out from underfoot, away from the heat of the kitchen. We also wanted to build a little enthusiasm for a plate of leftovers, prior to the ritual opening of wedding presents.

The wedding had been massive. The in-law men were Cossacks who whirled lightly around the dance floor. The in-law women were empresses less easily amused.

The bartender poured doubles all night long. There'd been an endless sea of wine on the tables, and someone played Ukrainian songs on a hammer dulcimer during supper.

We were given cups of borscht to drink. We ate little cabbage rolls and oven-roasted potatoes. We ate roast beef and breaded chicken and veal cutlets. We ate crepes which had been stuffed with sauerkraut, folded into neat squares and fried in butter. We ate something called meat-on-a-stick, which looked and tasted like its name.

At the head table, the bride picked at her food. Her normal diet is lettuce.

There'd been two desserts. The first, right after supper, consisted of coffee and trays of jam-filled, sugar-dusted dainties. That was just the warm-up. The second dessert came late at night, when everyone was polka'd into dizziness.

There was cheesecake. There were cream pies crowned with berries. There were watermelons skewered with fruit balls until they looked like hedgehogs. There was wedding cake and sponge cake and chocolate cake wheeled out on carts by women in white uniforms with hair-nets and florid pink complexions.

Afterwards, as the band was packing up, all the men with unbuttoned vests agreed the wedding was a brilliant success, and all the empresses beside them were content.

Now, in the bright light of the next afternoon, the bride walked with a heavy step. She appeared confused. Who are all these women in my house, she asked, and why are they trying to fatten me with endless buckets of food?

We sympathized, but I said it was the job of in-law women to lay out a feast and supervise its eating. For them a wedding is a culinary Superbowl—the more to eat, the better. The job of the bride is to smile and ask the older women how they make the cabbage rolls so small.

She walked in silence. I offered her some more advice. I said most weddings have very little to do with the bride and groom, and much to do with the relatives. A wedding warns the single men to settle down. A wedding reassures one's parents all is well at last. Finally, at a wedding, in-laws bored in marriage are reminded of their vows. With all this going on, the bride and groom are merely bystanders.

I said she ought to play her part as if she were a figure on the wedding cake. The bride considered this and kicked more leaves.

Back at the house, the men were smoking on the porch and swirling gin and tonics. Inside, women balanced plates and children darted underfoot. The sister of the bride ate meat-on-a-stick. I drank white wine from a tumbler, cut with ginger ale.

Across the room, I saw the bride smile wanly. She gathered herself and took an in-law woman by the elbow and pointed at an enormous vat of tiny cabbage rolls. I couldn't hear what she said, but the big woman smiled and blushed a modest pink.

As the day wore on, most of the presents got opened and the house filled up with pretty silver paper. Everyone was running out of steam, so the sister of the bride and I slipped out to a movie. By the time we got back, the guests were gone and the house had been thoroughly cleaned. The smell of cabbage rolls had been replaced by the scent of furniture polish, and all the footprints had been vacuumed from the carpets.

We were staying with them overnight, before they took their honeymoon. This was no intrusion. They'd been living together for some time.Tonight they were clearly tired. It had been a day of too many relatives, too much food, too much to drink, too many presents. In short, it had been perfect, and there were neat heaps of empty boxes to prove it.

They'd saved a few presents to open up when we got back. Mustering surprise for the last few gifts was work, but the night was not without amusement. We'd given them a stylized Italian fruit dish which the bride set out prominently, but upside down.

You remember that scene in *Bull Durham*? There is a conference on the mound during a baseball game to discuss what sort of present to buy for a player about to be married. After some discussion, the coach says candlesticks are a safe choice. Many of the bride's relatives saw that movie.

She opened her last gifts wearily. There was a salad bowl of exotic wood, with laminated forks. There were two glass salad bowls. There was another wooden bowl, this time ribbed, with matching ribbed salad forks.

Oh, boy, said the groom. More salad bowls. I guess the joke's on us, said the bride. Why's that, asked the bride's sister. Because we won't be able to palm off a salad bowl on you at Christmas, said the bride.

A restaurateur and food writer named George Rector started this business of the wooden bowl, and the ritual of hauling it out at table, rubbing it with garlic and tossing greens urbanely for your guests.

Back in the Thirties, he passed this off as a sophisticated and somehow European custom, but in fact it was nothing of the sort and no one did this anywhere in the world. However, the deception was a breakthrough. It made Americans aware that food was celebration. Provided you kept the bowl clean, and didn't let the garlicky oil turn rancid in the wood.

The bowls remind me of a joke which was a staple at weddings long ago.

A newlywed couple checks into a honeymoon suite. They are shown to their room by an unctuous concierge who is anxious to see that every comfort has been provided. They tip him quickly and usher him out.

But before the couple can consummate their bliss, they are interrupted by a knock at the door. It is the concierge delivering a bucket of champagne, compliments of the house. "Can I get you anything else?" No, thanks.

Five minutes later, in mid-kiss, there is another knock. It is the concierge, with a huge bouquet of flowers. "Can I get you anything else?" No, thank you.

And five minutes later, the concierge knocks again. This time, he delivers a complimentary basket of fruit. "And can I get you anything else?"

The groom, his collar open, is red in the face and breathing hard. Yes, there is one thing you can do for us, he says. You can bring us a honeymoon salad. The concierge is puzzled. A honeymoon salad is beyond the range of his experience. "I'll do it immediately, it will be an honour, but please tell me, what is a honeymoon salad?"

Oh, just lettuce alone, says the groom.

If you have to give a speech at a wedding, this will bring the house down. Corny works at weddings. Oh, and if you want a bowl for your honeymoon salad, I think I can get one for you cheap.

A TAR BABY'S NOTES

The roofers are at it again. I hear their propane burners every morning, throaty and insistent, boiling tar. The sound they make is the sound you'll hear where the road turns off to hell.

The roofers climb up scaffolds, hauling black pots overhead. Cauldrons of hot pitch steam on the walk. You have to look up as you pass them by. You have to watch your step. The roofers smoke and joke, and they don't give a damn for you or for roofs.

The tar they use is solid. It comes in short, hard tubes, like licorice allsorts, only bigger. Or else in lozenges a foot and a half square, black and thick and tacky as toffee. This is what they melt in their pots and mop over neighbourhood roofs.

A block of hard tar looks nearly good enough to eat. And depending on the wind, and the strength of your imagination, a pot of boiling tar looks good enough to swipe a taste from with your finger, like molasses. Don't.

I tried tar once. I got the idea from one of those "We were so poor…" stories I was told as a kid. You know the stories I mean. We were so poor we didn't have shoes, they said. We couldn't afford candy, they said, we used to suck on stones. We used to ball up tar when they paved the roads, they said, and chew on it like gum.

I was a skeptical kid, but one morning a work crew came and tarred our street. Tar as good as gum? If that were true, I was looking at miles of happy chewing. I checked right and left. There was no one around, and no one watching me from the window. I strolled to the edge of the road, and spat on my fingers to wet them. I bent down, rolled up a piece of tar and put it in my mouth.

Road tar tastes awful.

What did you expect? It tasted the way it smelled when the radiator on my uncle Dom's Plymouth blew. I thought I'd poisoned myself. My stomach turned. I spat it out, except for the bits that were stuck to my teeth.

What a stupid thing to do. I couldn't go in and brush it off with toothpaste—the black bits on the toothbrush would give me away.

I knew I was going to die. It was going to be horrible, a black death by agonizing inches, and no one would ever know why. I wasn't going to say a word. I didn't want to be laughed at while I was dying.

It was three days before I was certain I'd live.

Recently I remembered how dumb that felt. I had some licorice, the kind that tastes like salt and looks like those black triangles sticking down the corners of pictures in a book of family photos. I put some in my mouth, along with a piece of licorice toffee. (You can never have enough licorice in your pocket.) The texture was just about right. Like tar.

Then I walked to where the tar pot boys were working. And I took a whiff of what was boiling in the pot. Ah, the smell of the tar and the taste of licorice—for a moment I felt ten years old and stupid, and my tongue was black.

I can't wait to do it again.

TRICK OR TREAT

Every Hallowe'en, it seems I buy more candy than I need. I keep hoping to see long lines of little witches heading towards my house, along with ersatz ghosts and goblins, all of them holding the hands of their moms and dads. They do show up, of course. The trouble is, the lines are getting shorter and more straggly every year.

This sets up a dilemma—do I buy the good stuff so I can eat what I don't give away? Or do I buy those cheap neon-coloured suckers and deal them out by the fistful to the last few brats who show up two hours after everyone else has gone home?

It shouldn't matter, but it does. It's a ritual gift. I'm trying to appease the ghosts who roam the earth. I give them food so they won't steal into my house and cause me a year's worth of grief.

The hell it is. I do it so the little brats won't soap the windows.

Actually, some of these kids are not so little. Some of them are metalhead boys whose idea of a costume is a fright wig, a backwards baseball cap and a face full of their sister's lipstick and mascara. They say "Hallowe'en treats, please!" What they mean is "Stick 'em up!" Their girlfriends stand behind them in clots of perfumed aggression, holding plastic shopping bags and smoking.

I don't care about them.

My favorites are the little kids, the ghosts in pillowcases who can barely pronounce the word "Hallowe'en." They're too young to understand the concept. They stand wordlessly on the porch until somebody whispers "trick or treat" from a mile away on the sidewalk. I hate cute, but I make an exception for this.

You do, too. Admit it. You even get nostalgic for the sound of pennies rattling in a black and orange UNICEF box.

So go ahead. Buy a pumpkin and hollow it out. Stick it in the window with a candle. Good for you. Nice carving, scary face, snaggly teeth.

Waste of a good pumpkin.

But, just so the carving's not a total bust, rinse the gunk from the pumpkin seeds and simmer them in salted water for two hours. Leave them to dry completely on a clean tea towel. Then put them on a cookie sheet, sprinkle with a teaspoon of corn oil and bake at 350° for twenty minutes to half an hour. Eat 'em when they're cool.

What I want to know is, what is this thing with masks? I worked with a guy once who got nailed for armed robbery. He wore a mask, naturally. But one of the crimes he was charged with was hiding his face. This is something buried deep in the gut of common law; I guess we're not supposed to conceal who we are or what we look like, especially when we're holding people up.

Which reminds me. I went out for Hallowe'en once dressed as a money tree. Mom stuffed me in a cardboard cylinder and painted it like bark. She stuck willow twigs in the bark and pasted monopoly money onto the twigs. Good costume. Very original.

What did I know? I was young. I got laughed off the block. Neighbourhood toughs picked my leaves. And my candy was stolen by punks wearing masks.

I couldn't chase them in my trunk. Trees can't run. They can barely walk. I suppose it's a good thing I couldn't catch them. I wouldn't have known what to do. My imitation bark was worse than my bite.

So I broke my limbs off in frustration. I was a tree that cut itself down. This was an act of bush-town existentialism. Eight years old, and I'd already learned about the noise a tree makes falling in the forest. Did anybody hear me? I did. I still do. But it could have been worse. They could have come for me with chain saws.

Tell me this—is Hallowe'en the night before All Saints' Day or the night before All Souls' Day? I can never keep it straight. Do we pray for souls in purgatory, or do we assume that we're the ones in purgatory and hope that the wandering souls will pray for us?

All I know is, there'll be a lot of wandering souls this Hallowe'en. I refer to the straight guys who get a kick out of going to parties in drag. Maybe we should pray for them. These are guys who, if you asked them, would swear that Ru-Paul is a Montreal side-street. What is it with them, anyway? Don't they get it? And if they do get it, why don't they take the time to do their make-up properly? They give the real cross-dressers among us a bad name.

To each his own, I guess. We need our costumes in some earthy, fundamental way. We need to be what we're not for a night. We need to let our inhibitions run loose like dogs, and to hope like hell they come back when we call them.

I hope you're planning a Hallowe'en party this year. Why don't you set up a tub so the cross-dressers can bob for apples? The farmers will be grateful for the business. And you can tell your friends what the American wit, Dorothy Parker, once said.

She went to a Hallowe'en party, a gala replete with harvest cornucopias and lots of mixed drinks on the tables. Someone filled a tub with apples for bobbing. A crowd of swells gathered round, and there was general laughter and splashing.

"What are those people doing?" asked Miss Parker.

"Ducking for apples," someone told her.

"There, but for a typographical error," she said, "is the story of my life."

A CLOSE CALL

I used to think that a paid greeting was worthless, that any courtesy dispensed because it's on the job description was beneath contempt.

Airline stewards, the kids who greet you at the Gap, even those old retired boxers paid to nod and mumble at the highrollers going into Caesar's Palace—I used to think the lot of them were beneath contempt.

I've changed my mind.

One day recently, she felt a lump. She called her doctor on the telephone, and for once, she got through right away. There was no hesitation. The doctor scheduled her for an appointment with a specialist, and told her not to worry.

It was impossible not to worry. We had a day to consider that she might die. We talked about the odds. It might be nothing serious. And then we didn't talk. But even when we didn't, those odds were on our minds.

Her father had died earlier in the year. A colleague of hers had died recently, so quickly it was brutal. There were instances of cancer everywhere, and all the stories seemed to end the same way.

We hardly spoke on the way to the hospital. We understood that time might soon be divided into before and after this morning. There wasn't much to say.

And there was no comfort when we arrived. The hospital staff were dressed like inmates. We couldn't tell which of them were doctors or nurses, and which of them were cleaning up afterwards. We weren't greeted, and we were in desperate need of a greeting, anything to take the chill off.

The only people who seemed curious about our presence were other patients, or the relatives of patients. Misery loves company. The doctors or nurses, if that's what they were, looked at us blankly as they walked by. My hands were cold and so were hers. A decent hello from anyone would have given us some warmth, some strength.

The waiting room was a dull island. Patients, not all of them old, drifted past us. I had simple, unasked questions. Which of these people is about to die? And why is everyone looking at her? I held her hand.

We'd been considering her death for a day.

I waited while she went for X-rays. Two people in lab coats shared a private joke. Then one of them laughed and turned away, saying to the other, "You're dead meat." I winced.

A nurse picked up a chart. To no one in particular, but to everyone within hearing, she said "Expiry date 94/03." I flinched at the choice of words, even though I knew it was the date on someone's health card.

When she came back she looked pale. There was an envelope of X-rays in her hand. I glanced at the envelope and looked at her. "I don't know," she said.

We went off together to find the doctor's office. It took us forever to get there. The halls were marked with an algebra of meaningless directions.

Some young doctor with places to go and things to do, saw us standing in confusion. He stopped to give us directions, and smiled at us and wished us well. It was a welcome kindness. I still remember his face.

We found the office we were looking for, but the receptionist ignored us for so long it was rude. She preferred to take a phone call. She wouldn't look up from her forms. She shared a word with someone passing in the hall. I wanted to shout in her face to get her attention.

The doctor was another story. He was smiling, thoughtful and considerate, and the results were arrived at quickly. He looked her in the eye and came right to the point. The news was impossibly good.

We felt light-headed, the way you feel when you've missed being hit by a speeding truck. There was no cancer.

We stepped lightly going out the door, and I think I actually skipped on the way to the car. But there was little time for skipping. In spite of how afraid we'd been and how giddy we now felt, there were trivial things to do, work and calls to make and commitments that had to be met. We talked about what we'd have for supper. We wanted a celebration.

The rest of the day played out with sighs. I called her, she called me. We wanted to reassure ourselves of our good news.

At the end of the day, nothing looked worthwhile at the supermarket down the road. We got a pair of chops. The young people working the cash were turned out in green and white sweats, as if they were a team and the sweats were their uniform. This was new, and it made a cheerful atmosphere. These kids greeted us as if we mattered, and I was grateful to them. I still am.

The courtesy they were paid to provide, which I used to ignore and sometimes sneered at, became an aid to celebration. You're damn right we'll have a nice day! We'll have plenty of them, thanks.

Supper that evening was a simple thing. A bottle of wine forgotten in the cupboard turned out to be surprisingly good. We had penne with tomato sauce, the chops and a salad. Everything was seasoned with relief.

Comfort Me With Apples

In the photograph, the boy sits on a red sofa. In his hands he holds a pie plate, sticky with apple and brown sugar. The day is warm with the smell of cinnamon, and in the moment of the picture, all is sunny and right in the world.

The last of this pie is wealth beyond measure, the way sunlight is when you are three years old. I have the photograph. The boy is me.

The trouble is, I have no idea if the sensations I remember are real. I think I can feel the scratchy nap of the couch on my bare legs. I think I remember one of the springs of the sofa poking me where I sat. These may be embellishments. I may have created them to fit the photo.

What I remember may be nothing more than what I summoned to mind the last time I recalled the moment suggested in the picture. It doesn't matter. The memory is a comfort. So what if it's hand-tinted.

I dislike the phrase "comfort food," but the taste of apple pie makes me feel, for a moment, that nothing on earth can bring me harm.

I feel the same way about the taste of whiskey. It brings to mind an autumn night when the air was cool and the sky was dark and marked with stars. My baby brother had whooping cough; his lungs were choked with horrible, elastic gasps. He couldn't breathe.

I could hear my father and mother talking. Their voices came as hard whispers from the kitchen. Then I heard a door opening, and I got out of bed. It was three o'clock in the morning. I thought my baby brother was dying, and I went to find him.

The lights in the living room were on. My mother was still in the kitchen, drinking tea at the kitchen table. My brother was bundled in my father's arms out on the front porch, and I went to sit beside them in the night air. My father held my brother tightly and rocked him when he coughed.

Finally, when my brother wouldn't sleep, my father went inside and mixed some sugar with whiskey and warm water in a spoon and eased a bit of it into my brother's mouth. "It will help him sleep," my father explained. "I did the same for you when you had whooping cough." Eventually my brother settled down. For all I know, he may have been as drunk as an infant lord. But he survived the night.

I have other memories of my father and whiskey. They are less pleasant. But somehow, they all fade to the memory of that night when I sat beside him, and he cared for my baby brother.

Eventually, I applied the same remedy to my son during his one, terrible bout of whooping cough. Whiskey with sugar and warm water.

I haven't seen my son or my father for a long time. But the night air is cooling off, and the new apples are on the market. And I know that one of these sunny days I'm going into the kitchen to make an apple pie.

I'll eat the last piece of it right out of the pie plate.

And later on in the evening, I may take a glass of whiskey on the front porch. Cut with a little cold water. But no sugar. Some things are better left as memories.

Books on Food Cited

The following books have been instrumental in the preparation of these colums, either directly, as quoted in the text, or indirectly, as sources of inspiration and guidance:

A Dictionary of Superstitions edited by Iona Opie and Moira Tatem
Oxford University Press, 1989

The Frank Muir Book by Frank Muir
Stein & Day, 1976

Jane Grigson's Vegetable Book by Jane Grigson
Penguin Books, 1978

Jane Grigson's Fruit Book by Jane Grigson
Penguin Books, 1982

The Gold Cook Book by Louis P. DeGouy
Galahad Books, 1948

The Fanny Farmer Baking Book by Marion Cunningham
Alfred A. Knopf, 1984

Oranges by John McPhee
Macfarlane Walter & Ross, 1966

Fading Feast by Raymond Sokolov
E.P. Dutton, 1983

A Taste of Quebec by Julian Armstrong
MacMillan of Canada, 1990

On Food and Cooking by Harold McGee
Collier Books, Macmillan Publishing Company, 1984

Consuming Passions by Jonathan Green, ed.
Fawcett Columbine, Ballantine, 1985

The Rituals of Dinner by Margaret Visser
Harper Collins, 1991

The Fine Art of Italian Cooking by Giuliano Bugialli
Times Books, Random House, NY, 1977, 1989

The Kitchen Book/The Cook Book by Nicholas Freeling
David R. Godine, Boston, 1991

The Classic Italian Cookbook by Marcella Hazan
Ballantine Books, NY, 1973

Italian Home Cooking by Luigi Carnacina
Doubleday, 1972

The Renaissance of Italian Cooking by Lorenza de' Medici
Fawcett Columbine, 1989

Barbeque'n With Bobby by Bobby Seale
Ten Speed Press, Berkeley, CA, 1988

The Butcher by Alina Reyes
Methuen, 1991

Farewell, My Lovely by Raymond Chandler
Knopf, 1940

George S. Kaufman, An Intimate Portrait by Howard Teichmann
Dell, 1972

The Food of Italy by Waverly Root
Vintage Books, 1992

Finally, I would like to acknowledge a debt to the work of James Beard, MFK Fisher, Georges Simenon, and Rex Stout, from whom I learned at least as much about writing as I have about food.